Stories of Cali

CW01082671

Ella M. Sexton

Alpha Editions

This edition published in 2024

ISBN : 9789362923899

Design and Setting By
Alpha Editions
www.alphaedis.com
Email - info@alphaedis.com

As per information held with us this book is in Public Domain.
This book is a reproduction of an important historical work. Alpha Editions uses the
best technology to reproduce historical work in the same manner it was first
published to preserve its original nature. Any marks or number seen are left
intentionally to preserve its true form.

Contents

FOREWORD ....- 1 -

CALIFORNIA'S NAME AND EARLY
HISTORY ....- 2 -

THE STORY OF THE MISSIONS AND
OF FATHER SERRA ....- 5 -

BEFORE THE GRINGOS CAME ....- 11 -

THE AMERICANS AND THE BEAR-
FLAG REPUBLIC ....- 15 -

THE DAYS OF GOLD AND THE
ARGONAUTS OF 1849 ....- 18 -

MINING STORIES ....- 23 -

HOW POLLY ELLIOTT CAME
ACROSS THE PLAINS ....- 26 -

THE BUILDING OF THE OVERLAND
RAILROAD ....- 30 -

STORY OF THE WHEAT FIELDS ....- 33 -

ORCHARD, FARM, AND VINEYARD ....- 36 -

THE STORY OF THE NAVEL
ORANGE ....- 39 -

THE LEMON ....- 42 -

FLOWERS AND PLANTS ....- 44 -

THE BIG TREES AND LUMBERING ....- 48 -

OUR BIRDS ....- 53 -

OUR WILD ANIMALS ....- 58 -

IN SALT WATER AND FRESH ....- 63 -

ABOUT CALIFORNIA'S INDIANS ....- 70 -

THE STORY OF SAN FRANCISCO ....- 75 -

MEN CALIFORNIA REMEMBERS .... - 80 -

OUR GLORIOUS CLIMATE .... - 84 -

SOME WONDERFUL SIGHTS .... - 87 -

FOREWORD

To recount in simple, accurate narratives the early conditions and subsequent development of California is the purpose of this book. In attempting to picture the romantic events embodied in the wonderful history of the state, and to make each sketch clear and concise as well as interesting, the author has avoided many dry details and dates.

Several of the stories endeavor to explain the remarkable physical characteristics of California. The work to this end was rendered lighter by the hope that the reader might find the book merely an introduction to that larger knowledge of personal observation and inquiry.

But the writer's chief aim has been to interest the children of California in the beautiful land of their birth, to unfold to them the life and occurrences of bygone days, and to lead them to note and to enjoy their fortunate surroundings.

Among the many authorities consulted for the work, special acknowledgment is due to the historians, Theodore H. Hittell and H.H. Bancroft.

CALIFORNIA'S NAME AND EARLY HISTORY

A Spanish story written four hundred years ago speaks of California as an island rich in pearls and gold. Only black women lived there, the story says, and they had golden spears, and collars and harness of gold for the wild beasts which they had tamed to ride upon. This island was said to be at a ten days' journey from Mexico, and was supposed to lie near Asia and the East Indies.

Among those who believed such fairy tales about this wonderful island of California was Cortes, a Spanish soldier and traveller. He had conquered Mexico in 1521 and had made Montezuma, the Mexican emperor, give him a fortune in gold and precious stones. Then Cortes wished to find another rich country to capture, and California, he thought, would be the very place. He wrote home to Spain promising to bring back gold from the island, and also silks, spices, and diamonds from Asia. For he was sure that the two countries were near together, and that both might be found in the Pacific Ocean, or South Sea, as he called it, by sailing northwest.

So for years Cortes built ships in New Spain (or Mexico), and sent out men to hunt for this golden island. They found the Gulf of California, and at last Cortes himself sailed up and down its waters. He explored the land on both sides, and saw only poor, naked Indians who had a few pearls but no gold. Cortes never found the golden island. We should remember, however, that his ships first sailed on the North Pacific and explored Lower California, and that he first used the name California for the peninsula.

It was left for a Portuguese ship-captain called Cabrillo to find the port of San Diego in 1542. He was the first white man to land upon the shores of California, as we know it. Afterwards he sailed north to Monterey. Many Indians living along the coast came out to his ship in canoes with fish and game for the white men. Then Cabrillo sailed north past Monterey Bay, and almost in sight of the Golden Gate. But the weather was rough and stormy, and without knowing of the fine harbor so near him, he turned his ship round and sailed south again. He reached the Santa Barbara Islands, intending to spend the winter there, but he died soon after his arrival. The people of San Diego now honor Cabrillo with a festival every year. He was the sea-king who found their bay and first set foot on California ground.

About this time Magellan had discovered the Philippine Islands, and Spain began to send ships from Mexico to those islands to buy silks, spices, and other rich treasures. The Spanish galleons, or vessels, loaded with their costly freight, used to come home by crossing the Pacific to Cape

Mendocino, and then sailing down the coast of California to Mexico. Before long the English, who hated Spain and were at war with her, sent out brave sea-captains to capture the Spanish galleons and their cargoes. Sir Francis Drake, one of the boldest Englishmen, knew this South Sea very well, and on a ship called the *Golden Hind* (which meant the Golden Deer), he came to the New World and captured every Spanish vessel he sighted. He loaded his ship with their treasures, gold and silver bars, chests of silver money, velvets and silks, and wished to take his cargo back to England. He tried to find a northern, or shorter way home, and at last got so far north that his sailors suffered from cold, and his ship was nearly lost. Obliged to sail south, he found a sheltered harbor near Point Reyes, and landed there in 1579. Drake claimed the new country for the English Queen, Elizabeth, and named it New Albion. A great many friendly Indians in the neighborhood brought presents of feather and bead work to the commander and his men. These Indians killed small game and deer with bows and arrows, and had coats or mantles of squirrel skins.

NATURAL BRIDGE,
SANTA CRUZ.
Click photo to see full-sized.

Drake and his sailors repaired and refitted their vessel during the month they stayed at Drake's Bay. They made several trips inland also and saw the pine and redwood forests with many deer feeding on the hills; but they did not discover San Francisco Bay. On leaving New Albion, Drake sailed the *Golden Hind* across the Pacific to the East Indies and the Indian Ocean, and round the Cape of Good Hope home to England, with all the treasure he had taken. The queen received him with great honors and his ship was kept a hundred years in memory of the brave admiral, who had commanded it on this voyage.

During the next century several English commanders of vessels sailed the South Sea while hunting Spanish galleons to capture, and these ships often touched at Lower California for fresh water. Some of the captains explored the coast and traded with the Indians, but no settlements were made.

Then the Spanish tried to find and settle the country they had heard so many reports of, thinking to provide stations where their trading ships might anchor for supplies and protection. Viscaino, on his second voyage for this purpose, landed at San Diego in 1602. Sailing on to the island he named Santa Catalina, Viscaino found there a tribe of fine-looking Indians who had large houses and canoes. They were good hunters and fishermen and clothed themselves in sealskins. Viscaino went on to Monterey and finally as far north as Oregon, but owing to severe storms, and to sickness among his sailors, he was obliged to return to Mexico.

For a long time after this failure to settle upon the coast, the Spanish came to Lower California for the pearl-fisheries. Along the Gulf of California were many oyster-beds where the Indians secured the shells by diving for them. Large and valuable pearls were found in many of the oysters, and the Spanish collected them in great quantities from the Indians who did not know their real value.

In this peninsula of Lower California fifteen Missions, or settlements, each having a church, were founded by Padres of the Jesuits. But later the Jesuits were ordered out of the country, and their Missions turned over to the Franciscan order of Mexico.

With the coming of the Franciscans a new period of California's history began. Spain wished to settle Alta California, or that region north of the peninsula, and Father Serra, the head and leader of these Franciscans, was chosen to begin this work.

How he did this, and how he and his followers founded the California Missions you will read in the story of that time.

THE STORY OF THE MISSIONS AND OF FATHER SERRA

The old Missions of California are landmarks that remind us of Father Serra and his band of faithful workers. There were twenty-one of their beautiful churches, and though some are ruined and neglected, others like the Mission Dolores of San Francisco and the Santa Barbara and Monterey buildings are still in excellent condition. From San Diego to San Francisco these Missions were located, about thirty miles apart, and so well were the sites chosen that the finest cities of the state have grown round the old churches.

FATHER JUNIPERO SERRA
Click photo to see full-sized.

Father Junipero Serra was the president and leader of the Franciscan missionaries and the founder of the Missions. He had been brought up in Spain, and had dreamed from his boyhood of going to the New World, as the Spanish called America, to tell the savages how to be Christians. He began his work as a missionary in Mexico and there labored faithfully among the Indians for nearly twenty years. But as his greatest wish was to preach to those in unknown places he was glad to be chosen to explore Alta or Upper California.

Marching by land from Loreto, a Mission of Lower California, Father Serra, with Governor Portola and his soldiers, reached San Diego in 1769. Here he planted the first Mission on California ground. The church was a rude arbor of boughs, and the bells were hung in an oak tree. Father Serra rang the bells himself, and called loudly to the wondering Indians to come to the Holy Church and hear about Christ. But the natives were suspicious and not ready to listen to the good man's teachings, and several times they attacked the newcomers. Finally, after six years, they burnt the church and killed one of the missionaries. But later on there was peace, and the priests, or Padres as they were called, taught the Indians to raise corn and wheat, and to plant olive orchards and fig trees, and grapes for wine. They built a new church and round it the huts, or cabins, of the Indians, the storehouses, and the Padre's dwelling. In the early morning the bells called every member of the Mission family to a church service. After a breakfast of corn and beans they spent the morning in outdoor work or in building. At noon either mutton or beef was served with corn and beans, and at two o'clock work began again, to last till evening service. A supper of corn-meal mush was the Indians' favorite meal. They had many holidays, when their amusements were dancing, bull-fighting, or cock-fighting.

San Diego, called the Mother Mission, because it is the oldest church, is now also most in ruins. But its friends hope to put new foundations under the old walls, and to recap firm ones with cement, and preserve this monument of early California history.

MISSION CHURCH,
MONTEREY.
Click photo to see full-sized.

After Father Serra had started the San Diego settlement he set sail for Monterey. Landing at Monterey Bay, he built an altar under a large oak tree, hung the Mission bells upon the boughs, and held the usual services. The Spanish soldiers fired off their guns in honor of the day and put up a great cross. The Indians had never heard the sound of guns and were so frightened that they ran away to the mountains. The second Mission was built on the Carmel River, a little distance from the site of the first altar. This was called San Carlos of Monterey, and the settlement was the capital of Alta California for many years. It was also the Mission that Father Serra loved the best, and after every trip to other and newer settlements he returned to San Carlos as his home. This Monterey Mission is well preserved, and books, carved church furniture, and embroidered robes used in the old services are still shown.

At both San Diego and Monterey a presidio, or fort, was built for the soldiers. These forts had one or two cannon brought from Spain, and had around them high walls, or stockades, to protect, if it should be necessary, the Mission people from the Indians. The cannon were fired on holidays, or to frighten troublesome Indians.

All the Mission buildings were of brown clay made into large bricks about a foot and a half long and broad, and three or four inches thick. These bricks, dried in the sun, were called adobes, and were plastered together and made smooth by a mortar of the same clay. Then the walls were coated outside and inside with a lime stucco and whitewashed. The roof timbers were covered with hollow red tiles, each like the half of a sewer pipe, and these were laid to overlap each other so that they kept the rain out. The floors were of earth beaten hard, and the windows had bars or latticework, but no glass. The large church was snowy white within and without and had pictures brought from Spain and much carved furniture, such as chairs, benches, and the pulpit made by the Indians. One or two round-topped towers and five or six belfries, each holding a large bell, were on the church roof, and a great iron cross at the very top.

OLD SAN DIEGO MISSION.
Founded 1769.
Click photo to see full-sized.

Night and morning the Mission bells rang to call the Indians to mass or service, and chimes or tunes were rung on holidays or for weddings. These Mission bells were brought from Spain, and it was thought a blessing rested on the ship which carried them, and that shipwreck could not come to such a vessel. We read of one captain joyfully receiving the Mission bells to take to San Diego. When nearing the coast his vessel struck a rock, yet passed on in safety because, as he said, no harm could happen with the bells on board. On his journeys every missionary carried a bell with him for the new church he was to build. Father Serra's first act on reaching a stopping-place was to hang the bell in a tree and ring it to gather the Indians and people for service.

San Antonio, a very successful Mission, was the third one established, and it was in a beautiful little valley of the Santa Lucia Mountains. Every kind of fruit grew in its orchards, and the Indians there were very happy and contented, and in large workshops made cloth, saddles, and other things. San Gabriel, not far from Los Angeles and sometimes called the finest church of all, was the next to be built. This was the richest of the Missions and had great stores of wool, wheat, and fruit, which the hard-working Indians earned and gave to the church. The Indians, indeed, were almost slaves, and worked all their lives for the Padres without rest or pay. At San Gabriel the first California flour-mill worked by a stream of water turning the wheel, was put up. Some of the old palms and olive trees are still growing there.

San Juan Capistrano, founded in 1776, was one of the best-known Missions, for it had a seaport of its own at San Juan. Vessels came to its port for the hides and tallow of thousands of cattle herded round the Mission. The first fine church of this Mission was destroyed by an earthquake, and many people were killed by its falling roof. It was rebuilt, however, and still shows its fine front, and long corridors or porches round a hollow square where a garden and fountain used to be.

MISSION DOLORES.
Established 1776.
Click photo to see full-sized.

Old records tell us that Father Serra felt that there should be a church named in honor of Francis, who was the founder and patron saint of the

Franciscan brotherhood of monks to which these missionaries belonged. When Father Serra spoke of this to Galvez, that priest replied, "If our good Saint Francis wants a Mission, let him show us that fine harbor up above Monterey and we will build him one there." Several explorers had failed to find this port about which Indians had spoken to the Spanish. At last Ortega discovered it, and Father Palou, in 1776, consecrated the Mission of San Francisco. Near the spot was a small lake called the "Laguna de los Dolores," and from this the church was at last known as the Mission Dolores. But the great city bears the Spanish name of Saint Francis, or San Francisco. A fort was erected where the present Presidio stands, and later a battery of cannon was placed at Black Point. It is told that the Indians were very quarrelsome here and fought so among themselves that the Padres could get no church built for a year. In that part of San Francisco called the Mission, the old building with its odd roof and three of the ancient bells is a very interesting place to visit. There are pictures, and other relics of the past to see, and in the graveyard many of San Francisco's early settlers were buried. This was the sixth Mission of Alta California.

SANTA BARBARA MISSION.
Founded 1786.
Click photo to see full-sized.

The Santa Barbara Mission, where Franciscan fathers still live, has a fine church with double towers and a long row of two-story adobe buildings enclosing a hollow square where a beautiful garden is kept. One of the brotherhood, wearing a long brown robe just as Father Serra did, takes visitors into the church, and also shows them the garden and a large carved stone fountain. This church is built of sandstone with two large towers and a chime of six bells, and was finished in 1820. The Santa Ynez Mission was much damaged by the heavy earthquake that in 1812 ruined other Missions. Here the Indians raised large crops of wheat and herded many cattle. Over a thousand Indians, it is said, attacked this church in 1822, but the priest in charge frightened them away by firing guns. This warlike conduct so displeased the Padres, who wished the natives ruled by kindness, that the poor priest was sent away from the Mission. One of the early Missions was San Luis Obispo, where services are still held. It was specially noted for a fine blue cloth woven by the Indians from the wool of the Mission flocks of sheep. The Indians there also wove blankets, and cloth from cotton raised upon their own lands.

MISSION SAN LUIS REY.
Founded 1798.
Click photo to see full-sized.

San Juan Bautista, or St. John the Baptist, north of Monterey, had a splendid chime of nine bells said to have been brought from Peru and to have very rich, mellow tones. San Miguel had a bell hung up on a platform in front of the church, and now at Santa Ysabel, sixty miles from San Diego, where the Mission itself is only a heap of adobe ruins, two bells hang on a rude framework of logs. The Indian bell-ringer rings them by a rope fastened to each clapper. The bells were cast in Spain and much silver jewellery and household plate were melted with the bell-metal. Near them the Diegueño Indians worship in a rude arbor of green boughs with their priest, Father Antonio, who has worked for thirty years among the tribe. They live on a rancheria near by and are making adobe bricks, hoping soon to build a church like the old Mission long since crumbled away. The last of the Missions was built in 1823 at Sonoma, and proved very active in church work, some fifteen hundred Indians having been there baptized.

Father Junipero Serra died at more than seventy years of age, at San Carlos. During all his life in America he endured great hardships and suffering to bring the gospel to the heathen as he had dreamed of doing in his boyish days. A monument to his memory has been erected at Monterey by Mrs. Stanford, but the Missions he founded are his best and most lasting remembrances.

BEFORE THE GRINGOS CAME

This is the story Señora Sanchez told us children as we sat on the sunny, rose-covered porch of her old adobe house at Monterey one summer afternoon. And as she talked of those early times she worked at her fine linen "drawn-work" with bright, dark eyes that needed no glasses for all her eighty years and snow-white hair.

"When I was a girl, California was a Mexican republic," said the Señora, "and Los Gringos, as we called the Americans, came in ships from Boston. They brought us our shoes and dresses, our blankets and groceries; all kinds of goods, indeed, to trade for hides and tallow, which was all our people had to sell in those days. For no one raised anything but cattle then, and all summer long cows cropped the rich clover and wild oats till they were fat and ready to kill. In the fall the Indians and vaqueros, or cowboys as you children call them, drove great herds of cattle to the Missions near the ocean where the Gringos came with their ship-loads of fine things and waited for trading-days.

"For weeks every one worked hard, killing the cattle, stripping off their skins and hanging the green or fresh hides over poles to dry in the sun. When dried hard and stiff as a board the skins were folded hair-side in, and were then worth about two dollars apiece. The beef-suet, or fat, from these cattle was put into large iron kettles and melted. While still hot it was dipped out with wooden dippers into rawhide bags, each made from an animal's skin. When cold and hard these bags of tallow were sewed up with leather strings, and thus they were taken to Boston.

"So much beef was on hand at such times that not even the hungry Indians could eat it all while it was fresh. The nicest pieces were cut into long strips, dipped into a boiling salt brine full of hot red peppers and hung up to dry where the sunshine soon turned the meat into carne seca, or dried beef. We put it away in sacks, and very good it was all the year for stews, and to eat with the frijoles, or red beans, and tortillas, which were corn-cakes.

"All we bought from the Gringos was paid for with hides and tallow, so it was well, you see, children, that my father owned ten thousand cattle; for counting relatives and Indian servants, we always had more than thirty people on our ranch to feed and clothe. We raised grain and corn and beans enough for the family, but had to buy sugar, coffee, and such things.

"Did we have many horses, you say? Yes, droves of them, and we almost lived on horseback, for no one walked if he could help it, and there were almost no carriages or roads. Neither were there any barns or stables, for the mustangs, or tough little ponies, fed on the wild grass and took care of themselves. Every morning a horse was caught, saddled and bridled, and tied by the door ready to use. All the ladies rode, too, and I often used to ride twenty miles to a dance with Juan, my young husband, and back again in a day or so.

"Sometimes we went to the rodeo, where once a year the great herds of cattle were driven into corrals, and each ranchero or farmer picked out his own stock. Then those young calves or yearlings not already marked were branded with their owner's stamp by a red-hot iron that burnt the mark into the skin. After that the bellowing, frightened animals were turned out to roam the grassy plains for another year. We had plenty of feasting and merry-making at these rodeos, and a whole ox was roasted every day for the hungry crowds, so no one went fasting to bed.

"Those were gay times, my children," and Señora Sanchez sighed and sewed quietly for a while till Harry asked her if they kept Christmas before the Gringos came.

A CHRISTMAS GARDEN.
Click photo to see full-sized.

"Yes, indeed," she said, laughing, "we kept Christmas for a week, and all our friends and relatives were welcome, so that our big ranch-house was full of company. Indeed, some of the visitors slept in hammocks or rolled up in blankets on the verandas. Our house was built round the four sides of a square garden, with wide porches, where we sat on pleasant days. There was a fountain in this garden, and orange trees, which at Christmas-time hung full of golden fruit and sweet white flowers. On 'the holy night,' as we called Christmas Eve, we hung lanterns in the porches, and everybody crowded there or in the garden for their gifts.

"No, we had no Santa Claus nor Christmas tree, but my father gave presents to all, even to the Indian servants and their children. A fan or a string of pearls, perhaps, for my sisters, the young Señoritas; a fine saddle or a velvet jacket for my brother; and red blankets or gay handkerchiefs for the Indians, with sacks of beans or sweet potatoes to eat with their Christmas feast of roast ox or a fat sheep. Afterwards we danced till morning came, or sang to the sweet tinkle of the guitars. Well do I remember, children, when the good Padres, or priests, at the Mission forbade us to waltz, that new dance the Gringos had taught us to like. I recall, also, that the governor only laughed and said that the young folks could waltz if they wished. So at my wedding, soon after, when we danced from Tuesday noon till Thursday morning, you may be sure we had many a waltz.

"Pretty dresses, Edith? Yes, gay, bright silk or satin ones, with many ruffles on the skirts and wide collars and sleeves of lace, or yellow satin slippers and always a high comb of silver or tortoise-shell and a spangled fan. And we had long gold and coral earrings and strings of pearls from the Gulf, and, see!" as she pulled aside her neck-scarf, "here is the necklace of gold beads that was my wedding gift. We had no hats or bonnets, but wore black lace shawls, or mantillas, to church, or twisted long silk scarfs over our heads to go riding.

"You will think the gentlemen were fine dandies in those Mexican days, when I tell you that they often wore crimson velvet knee trousers trimmed with gold lace, embroidered white shirts, bright green cloth or velvet jackets with rows and rows of silver buttons, and red sashes with long, streaming ends. Their wide-brimmed sombrero hats were trimmed with silver or gold braid and tassels. They dressed up their horses with beautiful saddles and bridles of carved leather worked all over with gold or silver thread and gay with silver rosettes or buttons. Each gentleman wore a large Spanish cloak of rich velvet or embroidered cloth, and if it rained, he threw over his fine clothes a serape, or square woollen blanket with a slit cut in the middle for the head.

"Los Gringos used to laugh at the Mexican and his cloak, and not long after they came the 'Greasers,' as the Americans called the young men born here in California, began to wear the ugly clothes the Gringos brought out from Boston. And so the times changed, children, and our people learned to do everything as the Americans did it and to work hard and save money instead of dancing and idling away the time.

"And the bull-fights, Harry? Oh, yes, there was a bull-fight every Sunday afternoon, and everybody went, as you do to the football games. The ladies clapped their hands if the sport was good, or if the bull was killed by the brave swordsman. And if the men got hurt or the horses,—well, we only thought that was part of the game, you see. El toro, as we called the bull, always tried to save himself; and if he was savage and cruel, that was his nature, to try to kill his enemies. The gay dresses and the music was what I cared for, and then all my friends were there, also.

"But you must be tired of my old stories; is it not so, my children? No, you want to hear about the dances, you say? Well, every party was a dance; a fandango or ball, if it was given in a hall where everybody could come, but at houses where just the people came who were invited we called it only a dance. Every old grandfather or little girl, even, danced all night long, and the rooms were hung with flags and wreaths. All the Spanish dances were pretty, and the ladies with their gay dresses and mantillas, and the gentlemen in velvet suits trimmed with gold, made a fine picture. At the cascarone, or egg-shell dance, baskets of egg-shells filled with cologne or finely cut tinsel or colored papers were brought into the room, and the game was to crush these shells over the dancers' heads. If your hair got wet with cologne or full of gilt paper, everybody laughed, and you laughed too, for that was the game, you know. Ah, there was plenty of merry-making and feasting in those days, children," and Señora Sanchez sighed again and went on with her "drawn-work," while the bell in the old Mission church near by rang five o'clock, and we children ran home talking of those old times before the Gringos came to California.

THE AMERICANS AND THE BEAR-FLAG REPUBLIC

While Spain owned Mexico and the two Californias, the Missions were at their best and grew rich in stores of grain and in cattle and horses. Almost all the people were Spanish or Indians, and they lived at the Missions or in ranches near by. But when Mexico in 1822 refused to be ruled by Spain, Alta or Upper California became a Mexican territory, and, later on, a republic with governors sent from Mexico. The Mission Padres did not like the change, and thought that Spain should still own the New World. Before long it was ordered that the Missions should be turned into pueblos, or towns, and that the Padres were no longer to make slaves of the Indians. The missionaries were to stay as priests, and to teach the Indians in schools, but the Mission lands were to be divided so that each Indian family might have a small farm to cultivate. From that time the Missions began to decay and were finally given up to ruin.

Then Americans began to come in, the first party of hunters and trappers travelling from Salt Lake City to the San Gabriel Mission. All kept talking of the rich country where farming was so easy, and they wished to have land. But the Mexicans and the native Californians did not believe in allowing the Americans, as they called all the people from the Eastern states, to take up their farming lands and hunt and trap the wild animals. So there was much quarrelling. But the Americans still poured in, got land grants, and built houses.

In 1836, though Alta California declared itself a free state, and no longer looked to Mexico for support, Mexican rule still continued. The United States had wanted California for a long time, and had tried to buy it from Mexico. The fine bay and harbor of San Francisco, known to be the best along the coast, was especially needed by the United States as a place to shelter or repair ships on their way to the Oregon settlements. England also wanted this bay, but the Californians tried to keep every one out of their country.

Among the Americans who came overland and across the Rocky Mountains about this time was John C. Fremont, a surveyor and engineer, who was called the "Pathfinder." On his third trip to the Pacific Coast in '46 he wished to spend the winter near Monterey, with his sixty hunters and mountaineers. Castro, the Mexican general, ordered him to leave the country at once, but Fremont answered by raising the American flag over his camp. As Castro had more men, Fremont did not think it wise to fight, but marched away, intending to go north to Oregon. He turned back in the Klamath country on account of snow and Indians, as he said, and camped where the Feather River joins the Sacramento. It is almost certain that Fremont wished to provoke Castro and the Californians into war, and so to capture the country for the United States.

A party of Fremont's men rode down to Sonoma, where there was a Mission, and also a presidio with a few cannon in charge of General Vallejo. These men captured the place and sent Vallejo and three other prisoners back to Fremont's camp. Then the independent Americans concluded to have a new republic of their own, and a flag also. So they made the famous "Bear-flag" of white cloth, with a strip of red flannel sewed on the lower edge, and on the white they painted in red a large star and a grizzly bear, and also the words "California Republic." They then raised the flag over the Bear-flag Republic. Many Americans joined their party, but when the American flag went up at Monterey, the stars and stripes replaced the bear-flag.

At this time the United States and Mexico were at war on account of Texas, and Commodore Sloat was in charge of the warships on the Pacific Coast. The commodore had been told to take Alta California, if possible; so, sailing to Monterey, he raised the stars and stripes there in July, 1846, and ended Mexican power forever. The American flag flew at the San Francisco Presidio two days later, and also at Sonoma, Sutter's Fort, or wherever there were Americans. The flag was greeted with cheers and delight. Then Commodore Sloat turned the naval force over to Stockton and returned home, leaving all quiet north of Santa Barbara.

Commodore Stockton sent Fremont and his men to San Diego and, taking four hundred soldiers, went himself to Los Angeles, where the native Californians and Mexicans were determined to fight against the rule of the United States. General Castro and his men and Governor Pico, the last of the Mexican governors, were driven out of the country. Stockton then declared that Upper and Lower California were to be known as the "Territory of California."

In less than a month, however, the Californians in the south gathered their forces again and took Los Angeles. General Kearny was sent out with what was called the "army of the west," to assist Fremont and Stockton in settling the trouble. Peace was declared after several battles, and Kearny acted as governor of the new territory, displacing Fremont. At last, by the treaty which closed the Mexican war in 1848 Alta California became the property of the United States, and Lower California was left to Mexico.

From that time there was peace and quiet, and before long the discovery of gold brought the new territory into great importance. The rush to the gold mines brought thousands of men, and as no government had been provided for the territory, Governor Riley in '49 called a convention to form a plan of government.

This Constitutional Convention of delegates from each of California's towns met in Monterey. The constitution there drawn up lasted for thirty years, and under it our great state was built up. It declared that no slavery should ever be allowed here, and settled the present eastern boundary line.

The first Thanksgiving Day for the territory was set by Governor Riley, in '49. The first governor elected by California voters was Burnett, and in the first legislature Fremont and Gwin were chosen as senators. Congress at last admitted California into the Union by passing the California bill. On September 9, 1850, President Fillmore signed the bill.

Every year on the 9th of September, or "Admission Day," we therefore keep our state's birthday. At San Jose, in '99, a Jubilee Day was held in remembrance of the beginning of state government fifty years before.

THE DAYS OF GOLD AND THE ARGONAUTS
OF 1849

California has well earned her name of "Golden State," for from her rich mines gold to the value of thirteen hundred millions has been taken. Yet every year she adds seventeen millions more to the world's stock of gold. No country has produced more of this precious yellow metal that men work and fight and die for. The "gold belt" of the state still holds great wealth for miners to find in years to come.

Long, long ago people knew that gold was here, for in 1510 a Spanish novel speaks of "that island of California where a great abundance of gold and precious stones is found." In 1841 the Indians near San Fernando Mission washed out gold from the river-sands, and other mines were found not far from Los Angeles.

But James W. Marshall was the man who started the great excitement of '48 and '49 by finding small pieces of gold at a place now called Coloma, on the American River. Marshall, who was born in New Jersey, came to this state in 1847, and being a builder wished to put up houses, sawmills, and flour-mills. Finding that lumber was very dear, he decided to build a sawmill to exit up the great trees on the river-bank. He had no money, but John A. Sutter, knowing a mill was needed there, gave Marshall enough to start with.

So the mill was built, and when it was ready to run Marshall found that the mill-race, or ditch for carrying the water to his mill-wheel, was not deep enough. He turned a strong current of water into it, and this ran all night. Then it was shut off, and next day the ditch showed where the stream had washed it deeper and had left a heap of sand and gravel at the end of it. Here Marshall saw some shining little stones, and picking them up he laid one on a rock and hammered it with another till he saw how quickly it changed its shape. He was sure that these bright, heavy, easily hammered pebbles were gold, but the men working about the mill would not believe it. So he went to Sutter, who lived near at a place called Sutter's Fort, because his stores, house, and other buildings were built around a hollow square with high walls outside to keep off the Indians. Sutter weighed the little yellow lumps and said they certainly were gold.

The flood-gates between the mill-race and the river were opened again, and water ran through the ditch, washing more gold in sight. Sutter picked up enough of this to make a ring and had these words marked on it:—

"The first gold found in California, January, 1848."

Both Sutter and Marshall tried to keep what they had found a secret, but that was impossible, and soon people were flocking to the gold-fields. Then began a wild excitement known as the "gold-fever," and men left their stores and houses, gave up business, and left crops ungathered in a wild chase after nuggets of gold.

By December of 1848, thousands of miners were washing for gold all along the foot-hills from the Tuolumne River to the Feather, a distance of 150 miles. A hundred thousand men came to California during 1849, these Argonauts, or gold-hunters, taking ship or steamer for the long trip from New York by the Isthmus of Panama. Some went round Cape Horn, or else made a weary journey overland across the plains. "To the land of gold" was their motto, and these pioneers endured every hardship to reach this "Golden State."

PLACER GOLD MINING.
Washing with Cradle.
Click photo to see full-sized.

Then the miners, with pick, shovel, and pan for washing out gold from the gravel it was found in, started out "prospecting" for "pay-dirt." The gold-diggings were usually along the rivers, and this surface, or "placer," mining was done by shovelling the "pay-dirt" into a pan or a wooden box called a cradle, and rocking or shaking this box from side to side while pouring water over the earth. The heavy gold, either in fine scales or dust, or in lumps called nuggets, dropped to the bottom, while the loose earth ran out in a muddy stream. The rich sand left in pan or cradle was carefully washed again and again till only precious, shining gold remained.

So rich were some of the sand bars along the American and Feather rivers that the first miners made a thousand dollars a day even by this careless way of washing gold where much of it was lost. Then again for days or weeks the miner found nothing at all. He would wander up and down the cañons and gulches, prospecting for another claim, and dreaming day and night of finding a stream with golden sands, or of picking up rich nuggets. If he found good "diggings" he would build a rough shanty under the pines, and dig and wash till the gold-bearing sand or gravel gave out again. Sometimes he had a partner and a donkey, or burro, to carry tools and pack supplies. More often the Argonaut cooked his own bacon and slapjacks and simmered his beans over a lonely camp-fire, and slept wrapped in a blanket under the trees. If he had much gold, he would go to the nearest town, buy food enough for another prospecting tramp, and often spend all the rest of his money in foolish waste.

Sometimes a company of miners would build a dam across a river or stream, and turn it from its course, so they could dig out and wash the rich gravel in the river-bed. A flume, or ditch, would often carry all the water to a lower part of the river, leaving the bed of the upper stream dry for miles. In this kind of mining the "pay-dirt" was shovelled into long wooden boxes called sluices, and a constant stream of water kept the gravel and earth moving on out to a dumping-place. The gold dropped down or settled into riffles, or spaces between bars placed across the bottom of the sluices, and once a week the water was turned off and a "clean-up" made of the gold.

It was not long before the rivers, creeks, and gulches had all been worked over and most of the gold taken out. The miners knew that this loose gold had been washed out of the hills by the rains and storms of countless years. So some one thought of using a heavy stream of water to break down the foot-hills themselves and to carry the gold-bearing gravel to sluice boxes. This is called hydraulic mining and is the cheapest way of handling earth, as water does all the work and very little shovelling is needed. But since a strong water-power is necessary, a large reservoir and miles of ditches or wooden flumes must be built, so the first expense is large. The water usually comes from higher up in the mountains, and is forced under great pressure through iron pipes, the nozzle or "giant" being directed at the hillside, which has already been shattered by heavy blasts of powder. The water tears thousands of tons of earth and gravel apart, and the muddy stream flows through sluices, where the gold is left. In this kind of mining a great quantity of débris, or "tailings," must be disposed of.

For years this débris was washed into the rivers or on farming lands, filling up and ruining both, and leading to endless quarrels between farmers and miners. But at last the courts stopped hydraulic mining except in northern counties, where débris went into the Klamath River, upon which no boats could run and near which was little farming. But all the mines in the Sacramento and San Joaquin river-basins were idle till, in 1893, Congress appointed a débris Commission. These mining engineers issue licenses to work the mines when satisfied that the débris will be kept out of the rivers.

There are in the state many hundred thousand acres of gold-bearing gravel lands yet untouched, that could be worked by hydraulic mining.

In drift-mining the rich gravel is covered by hard lava rock thrown up by some old volcanic outburst. Tunnels are driven by blasting with dynamite, or by drilling under the rock to reach the gravel which usually lies in the buried channel of an old river. The long drifts, or tunnels, needed are very expensive and only mine owners with capital can work these claims.

Richest of all are the quartz mines, where beautiful white rock, rich with sparkling gold, is found in veins, or "lodes," cropping out of hillsides or dipping down under the earth. The great "Mother-lode" of our state runs like an underground wall across Amador, Calaveras, Tuolumne, and Mariposa counties and has been traced for eighty miles.

Some poor miner usually finds a ledge of quartz-rock and digs down the way the ledge goes. He puts up a windlass, worked by hand, over the well-like hole he has dug out, and hoists the ore out in buckets. But he soon finds, as the hole or shaft goes deeper, that he must timber the sides to keep them from caving in, that he must have an engine to raise the ore and a mill to crush the hard rock. So he sells out to a company of men, who put in costly machinery, deepen the shaft, and by heavy expenditure get large returns.

The quartz ledges dip and turn, so tunnels and cross-cuts are run to follow the golden vein, and all these are timbered with heavy wooden supports to keep the earth and rock from falling in on the men. The miners work in day and night gangs, using dynamite to break up the hard rock, and sending ore up in great iron buckets, or in cars if the tunnel ends in daylight, on the hillside. Sometimes the miners strike water, and that must be pumped out to keep the mine from being flooded.

The ore is crushed by heavy stamps, or hammers, and then mixed with water and quicksilver. This curious metal, quicksilver, or mercury, is fond of gold and hunts out every little bit, the two metals mixing together and making what is called an amalgam. This is heated in an iron vessel, and the quicksilver goes off in steam or vapor, leaving the gold free. The quicksilver, being valuable, is saved and used again, while the gold, now called bullion, is sent to the mint to be coined into bright twenties, or tens, or five-dollar pieces.

Some of the gold in the crushed ore will not mix with the quicksilver, and this is treated to a bath of cyanide, a peculiar acid that melts the gold as water does a lump of sugar. So all of value is saved, and the worthless "tailings" go to the dump. Even the black sands on the ocean beach have gold in them. In the desert also there is gold, which is "dry-washed" by putting the sand into a machine and with a strong blast of air blowing away all but the heavy scales of gold.

Though the Argonauts of '49 found much wealth in yellow gold, our "Golden State," on hillsides, in river-beds, or deep down in hidden quartz ledges, still holds great fortunes waiting to be found.

MINING STORIES

A large book might be filled with the stories told by the men who found gold in the early days. Their "lucky strikes" in the "dry-diggings" sound like fairy tales. Imagine turning over a big rock and then picking up pieces of gold enough to half fill a man's hat from the little nest that rock had been lying in for years and years!

And think of finding forty-three thousand dollars in a yellow lump over a foot long, six inches wide and four inches thick! This was the biggest nugget on record and actually weighed one hundred and ninety-five pounds. The next one, too, you might have been glad to pick up, as it held a hundred and thirty-three pounds of solid gold. Little seventy-five and fifty-pound treasures were common, and a soldier stopping to drink at a roadside stream found a nugget weighing over twenty pounds lying close to his hand.

It paid to get up early those days, also for a man in Sonora, while taking his morning walk, struck his foot against a large stone, and forgot the pain when he saw the stone was nearly all gold. Another man, with good eyes, got a fifty-pound nugget on a trail many people used all the time. One day, after a heavy rain, a man who was leading a mule and cart through a street in Sonora, noticed that the wheel struck a big stone; he stooped to lift it out of the way, and found the stone to be a lump of gold weighing thirty-five pounds. In less than an hour all that part of the town and the street was staked off into mining-claims, but no more was found. One of the largest of these nuggets was found by three or four men, who took it to San Francisco and the Eastern states, and exhibited it for money. They guarded the precious thing day and night, but at last quarrelled so that it had to be broken up and divided between them.

The first piece Marshall found was said to be worth about fifty cents, and the second over five dollars. Almost all, though, that was found was like beans or small seeds or in fine dust. No one tried to weigh or measure such gold more correctly than to call a pinch between the finger and thumb a dollar's worth, while a teaspoonful was an ounce, or sixteen dollars' worth. A wineglassful meant a hundred dollars, and a tumblerful a thousand. Miners carried their "dust" in a buckskin bag, and this was put on the counter, and the storekeeper took out what he thought enough to pay for the things the miner bought. A large thumb to take a large pinch of the gold-dust meant a good many extra dollars to the storekeeper in '48 and '49. Yet nearly every one was honest, and gold might be left in an open tent untouched, for there was plenty more to be had for the picking up. Those who would rather steal than work were driven out of camp.

Some of the "sand bars," or banks of gravel and earth, washed down by the Yuba River were so rich that the men could pick out a tin cupful of gold day after day for weeks. One place was called Tin-cup Bar for this reason. Spanish Bar, on the American River, yielded a million dollars' worth of dust, and at Ford's Bar, a miner, named Ford, took out seven hundred dollars a day for three weeks. At Rich Bar, on the Feather River, a panful of earth gave fifteen hundred dollars.

Yet the miners were seldom satisfied, but were always prospecting for richer claims. A man would shoulder his roll of blankets, his pick and shovel, with a few cooking things, and start off hoping to find some rich nugget, leaving a fairly good claim untouched.

The most extravagant prices were charged the miner for everything he had to buy. Ten dollars apiece for pick and shovel, fifty more for a pair of long boots, with bacon and potatoes at a dollar and a half a pound, soon took all his gold-dust to pay for. A dozen fresh eggs cost ten dollars, and a box of sardines half an ounce of gold-dust, which was eight dollars. There was no butter to buy, for any milk was quickly sold at a dollar a pint. The hotels charged three dollars a meal, or a dollar for a dish of pork and beans, and a dollar for two potatoes.

Lumber cost a dollar and a half a foot, but carpenters would not build houses when they could make fifty dollars a day by mining. As there was no lumber for the cabin floors, the ground was beaten hard and really made a good floor. In Placerville the houses were built along the bed of a ravine, and in sweeping these earthen floors some one saw gold-dust glittering, and found that rich diggings were under foot. Thereupon many of the miners dug up their cabin floors, and one man took about twenty thousand dollars in nuggets and gold-dust from the small space his cabin covered.

Very few women and children came to the mines in early days, and the first white woman to arrive in a camp had all sorts of attentions. Sometimes the town was named for the woman first in the place as Sarahsville and Marietta. If a lady visited a mining-camp, the men far and near would drop work and come in just to look at the visitor. One lady, who sang for the miners on her arrival in their town, was given about five hundred dollars' worth of gold-dust.

A child was a great curiosity, and any pretty little girl was sure to have a collection of nuggets or a quantity of gold-dust presented to her. The theatre and circus companies who visited mining-camps soon found out that a little child who could sing or dance was a great attraction. The miners used to throw a shower of money or nuggets at the feet of such little favorites as we throw flowers now.

As there were no women living here for some time, the men having left their families at home in the Eastern states, miners had to wash and cook and make bread for themselves. Men who had been lawyers or ministers at home, when there was no one else to do such things, washed their dishes or their red flannel shirts. On Sunday no one worked at mining, and the men baked bread and cleaned house, and Sunday afternoons they dried, patched, and mended their clothes. If a minister was in town, he held services on a hillside, or in the dining room of some shanty called a hotel, and all the camp came to hear him speak, or sang the hymns with him.

So the miners lived and worked and wandered along rivers and rough mountain trails on the west side of the Sierras, gathering up gold washed down by mountain streams. These Argonauts, or gold-seekers of fifty years ago, are almost all dead now, but the treasures they found made California known throughout the world. Their golden harvest has made the state richer than they found it, for they used the wealth to build cities, to cultivate farming-lands, and to plant orchards and vineyards where the mining-camps used to be.

HOW POLLY ELLIOTT CAME ACROSS THE PLAINS

This is the story of a little girl who in 1849 rode all the way from Ohio to California in an emigrant wagon. Polly Elliott has grandchildren of her own now, but she remembers very well the spring morning when her father came home and said to her mother, "Lizzie, can you get ready to start for the land of gold next week?" She hears again her mother saying, "Oh, John, with all these little children?" She says her father answered by swinging her, the eleven-year-old Polly, up to his shoulder and calling out, "Here's papa's little woman; she'll help you take care of them," as he carried her round the room, laughing.

This was "back East," as Polly Elliott, now Mrs. Davis, says,—in Ohio, where they had a pretty white house set round with apple and peach orchards all white and pink that May day. Her mother cried because they must leave the house, and because they had to sell all their furniture and the stock except Daisy, the pet cow, and Buck and Bright, the oxen, who were to draw the wagon. A round-topped cover of white cloth was fixed on the big farm-wagon. Then they piled into it their bedding in calico covers, a chest or two holding clothes and household goods, a few dishes and cooking things, and plenty of flour, corn meal, beans, bacon, dried apples and peaches, tied up in sacks.

Polly says she supposed the trip would just be one long picnic, while the four children thought it fine fun to "sit on mother's featherbed and go riding," as they said. So they started off for California. A long, long ride these emigrants had before them; a weary trip, plodding along day after day with the patient oxen walking slowly and the burning sun or pelting rain beating down on the wagon cover. There was a train of other wagons with them, some pulled by horses but more by yoked oxen, and the men walked beside the animals and cracked long whips. A few men were on horseback, but all kept together, for Indians were plenty and were often hiding near the road, watching for a chance to cut off and capture any wagons lagging behind the party.

Day after day, Polly told me, they travelled westward to the setting sun. They left the orchards and shady woods of Ohio and Indiana far behind them, and crossed the wide prairies of Illinois and Missouri also. When they came to rivers they drove through shallow fording-places, where Polly and the children used to laugh to see the little fishes swimming round the wagon wheels. Sometimes the rivers were deep, and the wagons were ferried over on a flatboat that was fastened to a wire rope, while oxen and horses swam through the water behind them. If it did not rain, the children and all were happy, and it did seem like a picnic. But Polly says she never hears the rain pouring nowadays as it did then, and that there were many times when they were wet and cold and miserable, and because the wood and ground were wet they could not even have a fire.

At night the teams were unhitched and the wagons left in a circle round a big camp-fire, where supper was cooked. Polly says her mother used to bake biscuits in an iron spider with red-hot coals heaped on its iron cover, and these biscuits with fried bacon and tea made their meal. They always cooked a big potful of corn-meal mush for the children, and this, with Daisy's milk and a little maple sugar or molasses, was supper and breakfast too. Then the women and children cuddled up in the wagons for the night, while men slept, wrapped in blankets, around the camp-fire or under the wagons, with one always on guard against danger from prowling Indians or wolves.

Every man or boy carried a rifle or shotgun, and killed plenty of game. Deer and antelope were always in sight after they crossed the Missouri River, and the meat was broiled or roasted over the coals of their campfire. Wild turkeys and prairie-chicken tasted much better than bacon, Polly said, and she learned to cook them herself.

When the emigrants reached Nebraska, they were in the "buffalo country," and great herds of big, shaggy, brown or black buffaloes were feeding on the grassy plains. The animals were larger than oxen, and the Indians depended upon the flesh for food and the thick, warm skins for robes or blankets. The emigrants shot thousands of buffalo cows and calves, and what meat could not be eaten at once was cut into long strips and hung in the sun or over the fire to dry. This was called "jerking" the meat. On jerked buffalo or venison and flour pancakes many emigrants lived all the way across. Game was so plenty and so easy to shoot, that by stopping a few days, a good stock of meat could be laid in while the oxen were resting. So they travelled through Nebraska, and for weeks and weeks saw nothing but long grass waving in the summer winds, and yellow sunflowers—miles and miles of sunflowers. Polly grew very tired of the hot sun blazing down on the close-covered wagon, and of the dust raised by the long wagon-train.

About this time she remembers that her father bought her a little Indian pony, and from that happy day the child rode beside the wagon, and could keep out of the dusty trail, or ride a little way off on the prairie, if she liked. The pony carried double very well, so a small sister or brother was often lifted on behind for a ride. One night the Indians, who were always prowling round and coming as near the wagon-train as they dared, frightened the horses and got away with ten of them. All the women and children cried, Polly says, for they were afraid the redskins would come back and kill them. In the morning Polly's father and some of the men found the Indians' trail and tracked them to a wooded cañon. The hungry thieves had killed one horse and were so busy feasting on it that the white men surprised them and shot all the Indians but two or three. The lost horses and Polly's pony whinnied to their masters from a thicket, where they were tied, and were taken back to camp.

On and on over the great plains of Wyoming the wagons carried these emigrants. Many found the trip grow tiresome, while the oxen and mules would often lie down in their traces and refuse to go any farther. A few days' rest, and the rich bunch-grass to crop soon set the stock all right, and the white-topped wagons crawled ahead again. Soon the emigrants saw blue, hazy mountains, far off at first, then nearer and nearer, till at last their road led through a pass between the peaks.

Then Polly remembers riding through Utah, with its queer red cliffs and high rocks carved in strange shapes by winds and weather; the stretches of sandy desert; and beyond those, grassy meadows and streams fringed with green willows. After a while Great Salt Lake lay sparkling in the sun and looking cool and blue. All around it were alkali deserts or wide plains, hot and dusty and white with salt or soda. The "prairie schooners," with their covers faded and burnt by the sun, went very slowly over these desert wastes, Polly thought, and Nevada, with its dusty gray sage-brush land on either side of the road, seemed not much better.

"Papa's little woman" had her hands full now; for her mother was so ill she seldom left the wagon. All the cooking fell to Polly's share, and then she would ride along for hours with a little sister on her lap and fat brother "Bub" behind her on the saddle-blanket, so that her mother might rest and be quiet.

But soon the clear green Truckee River ran foaming and fretting beside the road, and off in the west rose the snowy peaks of the Sierra Nevada Mountains. Then the people began to laugh and to sing, for they knew that California, the land of gold, was almost in sight and that their weary journey was nearly ended.

UPPER SACRAMENTO RIVER.
Click photo to see full-sized.

And one day they said joyfully to each other, "We are in California at last;" and it was a happy company that travelled down through the pines of the mountain sides and the oak trees of the foot-hills. Many emigrants left the train when they got to the great Sacramento River valley, and settled here and there to farming. Polly's father with others kept on to the gold-diggings and camped there. He built a log-cabin soon, for it was almost winter and time for the rains, and Polly says she was glad to have a house at last. They finally took up farming land near what is now Stockton, as gold-mining did not pay.

Mrs. Davis, who is straight and strong, and still a hard worker, says her five months' trip across the plains was almost like a long picnic after all, for she has forgotten many of the trying and disagreeable things.

THE BUILDING OF THE OVERLAND RAILROAD

The army of emigrants and gold-hunters who crossed the plains to California found it was a long and tiresome trip by wagon-train or on horseback. The oxen or mules would sometimes get so tired that they could go no farther; and because the food often ran short, there was much suffering from hunger.

The longest way of all to California was by sailing vessel from New York round Cape Horn, nearly nineteen thousand miles to San Francisco. The passengers paid high prices and were six months on the way. Those who came by the Panama route had trouble crossing the isthmus, where it was so hot and unhealthy that many died of fevers and cholera. The Pacific mail steamers connecting with a railroad across the isthmus at last shortened the time of this trip of six thousand miles to twenty-five days. For ten years all the Eastern mail came this way twice a month.

It was thought a wonderful thing when the "pony express" carried mail twice a week between St. Joseph, Missouri, where the Eastern railroads ended, and Sacramento. To do this a rider, with the mail-bag slung over his shoulder, rode a horse twenty-four miles to the next station, where a fresh pony was ready. Hardly waiting to eat or sleep, the rider galloped on again. Five dollars was often charged at that time to bring the letter railroads carry now for two cents.

So you will see that a railroad to join California to the Eastern states was a great necessity and had often been talked of. Several ways to bring the iron horse puffing across the plains and up the mountains with his long train of cars had been laid out on paper. The emigrants had found that the best highway from the Missouri River to California was to keep along the Platte River in Nebraska to Fort Laramie and the South Pass of the Rocky Mountains, then by Salt Lake, and along the Humboldt and Truckee rivers, crossing the Sierras at Donner Pass. Other roads were talked of, and Senator Benton of Missouri favored a nearly straight line between St. Louis and San Francisco. Some one, in objecting to this, said that only engineers could lay out a railroad, and such men did not believe a straight line possible. The senator answered: "There are engineers who never learned in school the shortest and straightest way to go, and those are the buffalo, deer, bear, and antelope, the wild animals who always find the right path to the lowest passes in the mountains, to rich pastures and salt springs, and to the shallow fords in the rivers. The Indians follow the buffalo's path, and so does the white man for game to shoot. Then the white man builds a wagon-road and at last his railroad, on the trail the buffalo first laid out."

For two or three years surveyors and explorers tried to find the easiest way to build this great overland road. Several railroad acts or bills were passed by Congress, and the California Legislature gave the United States the right of way for a road to join the two oceans.

The first railway in the state was opened in '56 from Sacramento to Folsom, a distance of twenty-two miles. This was built by T.D. Judah, an engineer who had thought and studied a great deal about the overland road so much needed to bring mail and passengers quickly from East to West.

A railroad convention, made up of men from the Pacific states and territories, was held in San Francisco in '59, with General John Bidwell, a pathfinder of early days, as the chairman. Here Mr. Judah gave such a clear and full account of the central way he had planned, that the convention sent him to Washington, D.C., to see the President, and to try to get Congress to pass a Pacific Railroad Bill. He had very little help in the East, but at last four men of Sacramento, Leland Stanford, C.P. Huntington, Mark Hopkins, and Charles Crocker, took an interest in Judah's plans, and in '61 the Central Pacific Railroad Company was formed. Mr. Judah went back to the mountains and studied the pines in summer and the winter snowbanks, to make sure of the easiest grades and the shortest and best way for the track-layers. He found that to follow the Truckee River from near Lake Donner to the Humboldt Desert, would mean the least work. The tunnels would be through rock, and he believed that snow might easily be kept off the track with a snow-plough.

His report pleased the company, and they sent him again to present the case at Washington. In '62 President Lincoln signed an act or bill to allow the Union and Central Pacific companies to build a railroad and a telegraph line from the Missouri River to the Pacific. In California the land for fifteen miles on each side of the way laid out was given to the railroad company, and two years was allowed them to build the first hundred miles of track.

Ground was broken for the Central Pacific the next year in Sacramento, and Governor Stanford dug up the first shovelful of earth. Then the work went steadily on, but it was hard to raise money. Stanford and his company carried the line forward as fast as possible. More land-grants were given, which doubled the company's holdings, and in '65 the road was fifty-five miles past Sacramento and had climbed over much difficult work.

The steamship owners, the express and stage companies were all against the railroad, and tried in every way to make people think that an engine could never cross the Sierras. Yet the grading went on, while an army of five thousand men and six hundred horses was at work cutting down trees and hills and filling up the low places. A bridge was built over the American River, and slowly but surely the track climbed the steep mountain-sides. Most of the laborers were Chinese, as white men found mining or farming paid them better.

In '67 the iron horse had not only climbed the mountains but had reached the state line, and the Union Pacific, which had been laying its tracks over the plains of the Platte River, began to hasten westward. The two railroads were racing to meet each other, and the Central sometimes laid ten miles of rails in one day.

Ogden was made the meeting-point, though at Promontory, fifty miles west of Ogden, the last spike was driven. A thousand people met at that place in May, '69, to see the short space of track closed and the road finished. A Central train and locomotive from the Pacific came steaming up, and an engine and cars from the Atlantic pulled in on the other side. Both engines whistled till the snow-capped mountains echoed. The last tie was of polished California laurel wood, with a silver plate on which the names of the two companies and their officers were engraved. It was put under the last two rails, and all was fastened together with the last spike. This spike, made of solid gold, Governor Stanford hammered into place with a silver hammer. East and west the news was flashed over the long telegraph line, that the overland railroad had been finished and that two oceans were joined by iron rails.

Now, while flying along in the cars so fast that the trip from Chicago to San Francisco takes but three days, it is hard to believe that little more than thirty years ago travellers in the slow-moving "prairie-schooner" took over five months to cover this same distance.

STORY OF THE WHEAT FIELDS

The Spanish Padres, as the Mission priests were called, taught the Indians to plough and seed with wheat the lands belonging to the church or Mission. They used a simple wooden plough, which oxen pulled. When the warm brown earth was turned up, the Indians broke the clods by dragging great tree branches over them. After the fall rains they scattered tiny wheat kernels and covered them snugly for their nap in the dark ground.

More rain fell, and soon the soaked seeds waked, and started in slender green shoots to find the sunshine, and day by day the stalks grew stronger and the fields greener. Higher and ever higher sprang the wheat, till summer winds set the tall grain waving in a sea of green billows. Have you ever watched the wind blow across a wheat-field? Over and over the long rollers bend the tops of the grain, that rise as the breeze goes on and bend low again at the next breath of wind.

When the hot sun had ripened the grain, and all round the white-walled, red-roofed Mission the fields stretched golden and ready for harvest, the Indians cut the wheat, and scattering the bundles over a spot of hard ground, drove oxen round and round on the sheaves till the wheat was threshed out from the straw. Then Indian women winnowed out the chaff and dirt by tossing the grain up in the wind, or from basket to basket, till in this slow way the yellow kernels were made clean and ready to grind.

A curious mill, called an arrastra, ground the grain between two heavy stones. A wooden beam was fastened to the upper stone, and oxen or a mule hitched to this beam turned the stone as they walked round. The first flour-mill worked by water was put up at San Gabriel Mission, and it was thought a wonderful thing indeed.

Even in those early days California wheat was known to be excellent, and many ships came on the South Sea, as they then called the Pacific Ocean, to load with grain for Mexico or Boston or England. Since that time our state has fed countless people, and over a million acres of valley and hill lands are green and golden every year with food for the world. To Europe, to the swarming people of China, Japan, and India, to South Africa and Australia, our grain is carried in great ships and steamers, and hungry nations in many lands look to us for bread.

For a long time after the Mission days, all the grain had to be hauled to the rivers or sea-coast for shipping. Then the overland railroad was finished, and within the next fifteen years an additional two thousand miles of railways were built in California, and nearly every mile opened up rich wheat land that had never been cultivated. Soon great wheat ranches stretched far over the dry, hot valley plains.

The ground is ploughed and seeded after November rains, and all winter the tender blades of grain grow greener and stronger day by day March and April rains strengthen the crop wonderfully, and June and July bring the harvest-time. As no rain falls then, the ripe wheat stands in the field till cut, and afterward in sacks without harm. All the work except ploughing is done by machinery, and this makes the wheat cost less to raise, since a machine does the work of many men and the expense of running it is small.

Some of the ranches have three or four thousand acres in wheat, and it may interest you to know how such large farms are managed. The ploughing is done by a gang-plough, as it is called, which has four steel ploughshares that turn up the ground ten inches deep. Eight horses draw this, and as a seeder is fastened to the plough, and back of the plough a harrow, the horses plough, seed, harrow, and cover up the grain at one time. There the seed-wheat lies tucked up in its warm brown bed till rain and sunshine call out the tiny green spears, and coax them higher and stronger, and the hot sun of June and July ripens the precious grain.

Then a great machine called a "header and thresher" is driven into the field and sweeps through miles and miles of bending grain, cutting swaths as wide as a street, and harvesting, threshing, and leaving a long trail of sacked wheat ready to ship on the cars. Thirty-six horses draw the header, and five or six men are needed to attend to this giant, who bites off the grain, shakes out the kernels, throws them into sacks and sews them up, all in one breath, as you might say. The harvesters work from daylight to dusk, and three-fourths of our wheat crop is gathered in this way.

Much golden straw is left, besides that which the "headers" burn as fuel, and farmers stack this straw for cattle to nibble at. The stock feed in the stubble fields, too, and strange visitors also come to these ranches to pick up the scattered grains of wheat. These strangers are wild white geese, in such large flocks that when feeding they look like snow patches on the ground. They eat so much that often they cannot fly and may be knocked over with clubs. In the spring these geese must be driven away by watchmen with shot-guns to keep them from pulling up the young grain.

The largest single wheat-field in California is on the banks of the San Joaquin River, in Madera County. This covers twenty-five thousand acres and is almost as flat as a floor. It is nearly a perfect square in shape, and each side of the square is a little over six miles long. There are no roads through this solid stretch of grain. Two hundred men, a thousand horses, and many big machines are needed to work this wheat-field.

Some of the big harvesters that cut and thresh the wheat are drawn by a traction-engine instead of horses. In running a fifty-horse-power engine high-priced coal had to be burnt but now the coal grates are replaced by petroleum burners, and crude coal-oil is the cheap fuel. This does not make sparks to set the fields on fire like burning coal or straw and so is safer to use.

On large ranches wheat can be grown for less than a cent a pound, while it has brought two cents or double the money when sold. But there are not always good crops, as the grain needs plenty of moisture in the spring when rains are uncertain.

The wheat crop of the state has fallen off of late to less than half the yield of earlier years, but the deep, rich valley soil still grows grain enough to feed hungry people in Europe, Asia, and Africa, as well as in our own Union. Great quantities are taken in large four-masted ships to Liverpool, England, and there made into American flour. Our own flour-mills turn out thousands of barrels of flour, and this travels far, too. The first thing picked up in Manila after Admiral Dewey's victory was a flour sack with a California mill mark.

It would need a long, long story to tell how far from home and into what strange places the yellow kernels of California wheat sometimes travel, or to picture the odd people who depend upon us for food.

ORCHARD, FARM, AND VINEYARD

Long ago the Mission Fathers taught the Indians to plant and to take care of vines and fruit-trees. They built water-works to bring life to the thirsty trees in the dry summers, and to grow oranges, limes, and figs, as well as peaches, apricots, and apples. They trained grape-vines over arbors and trellises round the Mission buildings, and from the small, black grapes made wine. Olive trees and date-palms did well at the southern settlements. But most of these orchards died when the Mission Fathers were no longer allowed to make the Indians work for the church property, though a few old palms and olive trees are still standing.

During Mexican days each ranch owner raised enough grain or corn and beans for his own family but planted no fruit, or but little, while the Americans who came to seek gold thought farming a slow way of making a living. People soon found out, however, that our fine climate and rich soil made good crops almost certain, and there was such demand for fruit and farm products that more and more acres were cultivated each year.

Our leading industry now is farming and fruit-growing, and California's delicious fresh or cured fruit is sent all over the world. Large amounts of barley and hops are shipped from here to Europe, and our state produces almost all the Lima beans used in the country.

The citrus fruits, as oranges, lemons, and pomelos, or "grape-fruit," are called, grow in the seven southern counties, or in the foothills on the western slope of the Sierras. The trees cannot endure frost and must be irrigated in the summer. Orange trees are a pretty sight, with their shining green leaves, white, sweet-smelling flowers, and the green or golden fruit. About Christmas-time, when oranges ripen, both blossoms and fruit may be picked from the same tree. Los Angeles and Orange County grow most oranges, but San Diego is first in lemon culture. Half a million trees in that county show the bright yellow fruit and fragrant blossoms every month in the year. The other southern counties also raise lemons by the car-load to send east, or for your lemonade and lemon pies at home.

There, too, the olive grows well, that little plum-shaped fruit you usually see as a green, salt pickle on the table. The Mission Fathers brought this tree first from Spain, where the poor people live upon black bread and olives. Olives are picked while green and put in a strong brine of salt and water to preserve them for eating. Dark purple ripe olives are also very good prepared the same way. Did you know that olive-oil is pressed out of ripe olives? The best oil comes from the first crushing, and the pulp is afterwards heated, when a second quality of oil is obtained. Olive trees grow very slowly, and do not fruit for seven years after they are planted. But they live a hundred years, and bear more olives every season.

The black or purple fig which grew in the old Mission gardens bears fruit everywhere in the state. Either fresh and ripe, or pressed flat and dried, it is delicious and healthful. White figs like those from abroad have been raised the last few years, and it is hoped in time to produce Smyrna figs equal to the imported.

While peach orchards blossom and bear fruit six months of the year in the south, most of this pretty pink-cheeked fruit grows in the great valleys, or along the Sacramento River. Pears also show their snowy blossoms and yellow fruit in the valleys and farther north. The Bartlett pear is sent to all the Eastern states in cold storage cars kept cool by ice, and also to Europe.

The finest apricots are those of that wonderful southern country, miles and miles of orchards lying round Fresno especially. Yet the valleys and foot-hills produce plenty, and in the old mining counties very choice fruit ripens. Apples like the high mountain valleys, where they get a touch of frost in winter, though there is a cool section of San Diego County where fine ones are raised. Cherries do well in the middle and valley regions, the earliest coming from Vacaville, in Solano County.

Grapes grow throughout the state, though the famous raisin vineyards, where thousands of tons are dried every year, are around Fresno. Most of the raisins are dried in the sun, but in one factory a hundred tons of grapes may be dried at one time by steam. The raisins are seeded by machinery, and packed in pretty boxes to send all over the coast, and through the states, where once only foreign raisins were used. Many vineyards in the southern part and middle of the state grow only wine grapes, California wines, champagne, and brandy having a wide use.

Great quantities of fresh fruits are used in the state or sent away, while the canneries put up immense amounts, also. Canned fruit reaches many consumers, but it is expensive. Our cured or dried fruit, however is so cheap and so good that millions of pounds are prepared every year. Such fruit ripens on the tree and so keeps all its fine flavor. It is then dried in the sunshine, which not only fits it for long keeping but turns part of it to sugar. Apricots, peaches, pears, and cherries are usually cut in halves or stoned before drying. Prunes are first on the list of cured fruits, and they seem the best to use as food. The ripe prunes are dipped into a boiling lye to make the skin tender, then rinsed and spread in the sun a day or two. They are then allowed to "sweat" to get a good color, are next dipped in boiling water a minute or two, dried, and finally graded, a certain number to the pound, and packed in boxes or sacks.

Several kinds of nuts grow well in the state. All the so-called "English" walnuts, with their thin shells, are raised in the south, Orange County furnishing half the amount we market. Peanuts and almonds are a good crop there, also, though almond groves are in all parts of the state. Both paper and thick-shelled almonds are usually bleached, or whitened, with sulphur smoke to improve their color.

Santa Barbara and Ventura are the bean counties of the state, and send Lima beans away by train-loads, while Orange County grows celery for the Eastern market. Very high prices are received for this celery and other vegetables sent from California during the winter season when fields are covered with snow in the East. And did you know that the state produces a great deal of sugar? Tons and tons of sugar-beets are grown throughout the farming lands, and harvested in September. When the juice of these crushed beets is boiled and refined, it makes a sugar exactly like cane sugar and much cheaper. One-fifth of the beet is sugar, it is said. Even the dry, worthless mountain sides are valuable to the bee-keeper. The bees make a delicious honey from the wild, white sage, which grows where nothing else will live. This sage honey brings the very highest price.

Oats are raised in the coast counties, and corn in the valleys, but owing to cool nights and dry air the corn seldom makes a good crop. Orange County, however, claims corn with stalks twenty feet high and a hundred bushels to the acre. In the south, also, that wonderful forage-plant, alfalfa, will produce six crops a year by irrigation and give a ton or more to the acre at each cutting. Along the upper Sacramento River stretch the great hop-fields full of tall vines covered with light-green tassels. At hop-picking season many families have a month's picnic, children and all working day after day in the fields and pulling off the fragrant hops. Indians, too, are among the best hop-pickers. The dried hops are bleached with sulphur, baled, and in great quantities sent to Liverpool, where with California barley they are used in brewing malt liquors.

An odd crop is mustard, and at Lompoc, in Santa Barbara County, enough for the whole country is grown. Both brown and yellow mustard is cultivated, and the little seeds, almost as fine as gunpowder, are sold to spice-mills and pickle-factories.

Whole farms are taken up with the production of flower-seeds or bulbs, with acres and acres of calla-lilies, roses, carnations, and violets. The tall pampas-grass, with its long feathery plumes, gives a profitable crop. Indeed, one can scarcely name a fruit, flower, or tree that will not thrive and grow to perfection in our mild climate and rich soil.

THE STORY OF THE NAVEL ORANGE

Who has not enjoyed a juicy navel orange, while wondering at its peculiar shape and lack of troublesome seeds? Yet few people know that this particular variety has brought millions of dollars into our state and made orange growing our third greatest industry.

Read this story of the seedless orange, this "golden apple of California," which was first cultivated by Luther Tibbets, of Riverside, and learn how Southern California has profited by its navel orange crops.

Nearly thirty years ago Mr. Tibbets came from New York to this state and took up free government land near what is now the beautiful city of Riverside. He was one of the half-dozen pioneer fruit-growers of that region, and had noticed at the San Gabriel Mission how well orange trees grew there. His wife and daughter waited in Washington, D.C., until a home should be ready here for them, and they often sent Mr. Tibbets plants and seeds from the Department of Agriculture. To this Department and its gardens in Washington, many curious plants are forwarded from other countries for growing and experiment in the United States. New kinds of grain or fruits are carefully cultivated and watched by the Department, and from it farmers can always get seeds or cuttings to try on their own farms.

Mrs. Tibbets often visited the Department gardens, and in 1873 she wrote to her husband that she could get him some fine orange trees if he would promise the government to take great care of them and to keep them apart from other trees till they fruited. Of course he agreed to give them special attention, and therefore that December he received three small, rooted orange trees. A cow chewed up one of these, but for five years the others were watched and tended. Then sweet white blossoms appeared on each little tree, and afterwards two oranges, like hard green bullets at first. Finally, in January, 1879, Mr. Tibbets picked four large, well-flavored, golden oranges, the first seedless ones ever grown outside of Brazil.

From the hot swamps of the tropical country at Bahia the United States Consul had sent six cuttings of this peculiar orange to be planted in the Washington gardens. All died but the two at Riverside. In 1880 they bore half a bushel of fruit, and the new seedless oranges were talked of throughout Southern California. The other orange growers had been cultivating "seedlings," trees which bore smaller fruit, with many bitter seeds and a thick skin. Many of these growers now cut back their seedlings to bare limbs, and grafted the new orange on these branches. This is called "budding," and is done by cutting off a thin slip of bark with a tiny folded-up leaf-bud on it, inserting the graft in the branch to be budded and securing it there with wax to keep the air out. The little bud drinks in sap from the tree stem, and grows and blossoms true to its own mother tree.

There were few orange groves then, but soon nearly all were budded to the new kind, seventy-five acres being so changed on the Baldwin Ranch; and when these trees began to bear, some five years afterwards, people were much excited over the seedless fruit.

AN ORANGE TREE WITH
FRUIT AND BLOSSOMS.
Click photo to see full-sized.

Such high prices were paid for these oranges at first, that orange growing boomed all over Southern California. People thought their fortunes were made when they set out a few acres of small budded trees they had paid a dollar or more apiece for. Whole towns sprang up in dry treeless valleys where only cattle and sheep had pastured, and land worth only twenty-five dollars an acre before the orange excitement, sold quickly for eight hundred and a thousand when planted with trees. The towns of Pomona, Redlands, Monrovia, and others in the orange localities were unknown before 1885, and grew to several thousand population in a few years. Everybody talked of the great profit in orange growing, and people who had nurseries of young trees grown from navel buds made fortunes.

At this day thousands of acres of seedless oranges are in full bearing and no one buys the old kinds. Hundreds of car-loads of the seedlings are not even picked, and ninety per cent of the eighteen thousand car-loads which make the season's orange crop are navel oranges. Over forty-five millions of dollars are now invested in the growing and marketing of this remarkable fruit.

At Riverside, the home of the orange, the two original Washington navel trees still stand. Mr. Tibbets guarded them for years, had them fenced with high latticework, and seldom allowed any one to touch them. He refused ten thousand dollars for them, since for months he sold hundreds of dollars' worth of buds from these parent trees. These two trees and their large family have caused thousands of people to come to the state, and have built up Southern California wonderfully.

THE LEMON

For many years people who use that sour but necessary fruit, the lemon, thought that only the little yellow ones which came from the far-away island of Sicily were good. The men who import foreign fruits always said so; and in spite of the fact that the larger California lemon was more acid, of as good flavor, smooth skinned, and golden, people believed the Mediterranean groves produced the best. But, at last, our warm, dry air, good soil, and plenty of water, together with care and skill while growing and packing, have made California lemons the most in demand. These lemons keep well, and bear shipping and long journeys better than the imported fruit.

Citrus fruits, as the orange and lemon are called, do well in all the southern counties, and San Diego County boasts of not only the largest lemon grove in California, but in the world. This is a thousand-acre tract overlooking San Diego Bay and cultivated by the Chula Vista colony. It was once a pasture given up to wandering bands of cattle and sheep. There was little water, and no one ever thought these dry mesa lands would one day be a beautiful garden spot, green with the shining lemon leaves, and golden with fruit.

A company was formed to develop this forty-two square miles of land, and to get water for irrigation, since all the trees must have little streams of water round their thirsty roots three or four times during the dry summer. A great dam was constructed on the Sweetwater River, near Chula Vista, and a reservoir built. Water was piped from this to the lemon groves, which are about a hundred feet below the reservoir, and from May to September the trees are irrigated. This is done by ploughing furrows on each side of a row of trees and turning small rills of water slowly down them till the ground is soaked around the tree roots. No one thought the great reservoir would ever be empty, but two winters with but little rain made it necessary to put down many wells in the dry bed of the Sweetwater River, and from these a strong steady flow of millions of gallons is pumped into the water pipes. So this great lemon orchard is always sure of water enough, returning the gift later in generous golden measure.

One may pick lemon blossoms, ripe and green fruit every month in the year from the same tree, but most of the crop ripens from November to June.

Lemons are carefully cut from the tree, and usually picked by size, a ring being slipped over them, without regard to their ripeness. They grow so thick on the tree that a man can pick more than twenty boxes a day. In preparing it for market the fruit "sweats," as it is called, in airy boxes, for a month in winter and ten days in summer, and ripens and colors during this process. Then each lemon is wiped dry and clean, wrapped separately in tissue-paper, and packed for shipment. The cost of a box of lemons from the tree to the railroad is about thirty-five cents.

Thousands of car-loads are shipped to the Eastern and Middle states, while the Pacific Coast is a never-failing market.

Small, imperfect, and bruised fruit goes to the citric acid factory near the packing-houses. From these oil of lemon, lemon sugar, and clear green citric-acid crystals are made, and the crushed waste is returned to the grove and ploughed in about the trees as a fertilizer.

FLOWERS AND PLANTS

"When California was wild," says John Muir, "it was one sweet bee-garden throughout its entire length, and from the snowy Sierra to the ocean."

There were so many yellow poppies in this great unfenced garden, that the Spanish sailing along the coast called it the "Land of Fire" from the golden flowers covering the hills. Near Pasadena, in Southern California, these poppy fields may still be seen glowing so brightly in the sun that you do not wonder at the name "Cape Las Flores," or Flower Cape, which the sailors also gave to this part of the country.

The poppy is our best-known wild flower, planted by Mother Nature before white men ever visited these shores. When the Spanish settled here they called the poppy *copa de oro*, or cup of gold. The gold hunters spoke of it as the California gold flower, and sent the pressed poppies home in their letters. But its correct name is the Eschscholtzia (esh-sholt'si-a), from the name of a German botanist and naturalist, who studied the plant and wrote about it almost a hundred years ago.

From February to May the poppies are most plentiful, but a few may be found almost every month in the year. Have you noticed the finely cut green leaves, and the pointed green nightcap that covers each bud till the morning sunshine coaxes off the cap and unfolds the four satiny golden petals? The flowers love the sun and close up on dark, cloudy days, or if brought into the house. But put them in a sunny window the next morning, and you may watch the cups of gold open to the light.

Some of the poppies are a deep orange-color, while others are a pale yellow. And as you walk through the fields you may pick a hundred at each step, so thick do the plants grow. The wild bees find a yellow dust called pollen or "bee-bread" in the poppy, the same golden powder that rubs off on your nose, when you put it too close to this cup of gold or to lilies.

Then in this "unfenced garden" were also the baby blue-eyes, whose pretty pale-blue blossoms come early in the spring, each one with a drop of honey at the foot of its honey path, as the black lines on its petals are called.

Can you name twenty kinds of wild flowers? Around San Francisco and the bay counties you will count, after the poppy and baby blue-eyes, the shining yellow buttercup, the blue and yellow lupines that grow in the sand, the tall thistle whose sharp, prickly leaves and thorny red blossoms spell "Let-me-alone," the blue flag-lilies and red paint-brush, yellow cream-cups, and wild mustard, and an orange pentstemon. These with many yellow compositæ or flowers like the dandelion, you will find growing on the windy hills and dry, sunny places. Hiding away in quiet corners are the blue-eyed grass, and a wild purple hyacinth, the scarlet columbine swinging its golden tassels, shy blue larkspur, a small yellow sunflower, and wild pink roses. Among the ferns in shady, wet nooks are white trilliums and a delicate pink bleeding-heart, while the wild blue violets and yellow pansies love the warm, rocky hillside.

Mariposas, or butterfly tulips of many colors, grow in the foot-hills and mountains. Perhaps our most beautiful wild flowers are the lilies, of which we have over a dozen kinds. In the redwood forests there is a tall, lovely pink lily, and many brown-spotted yellow tiger-lilies. Up in the mountain pines a snowy white Washington lily sometimes covers a mountain side with its tall stems bearing dozens of sweet waxen blossoms. In the wet, swampy places bright red, and many small orange lilies bloom in late summer.

In the high Sierras are found strange and pretty blossoms unlike the flowers of valleys and sea-coast. There you will see the mountain-heather with pink, purple, or dainty white bells, the goldenrod, and gentians blue as the sky. Strangest of all is the snow-plant. This curious thing sends up a thick, fleshy spike a foot or so in height and set closely with bright scarlet flowers. It grows where the snow has just melted round the fir trees, and leaf, stem, and blossom are all the same glowing red.

Most of the valley and coast wild-flowers bloom and ripen their seeds before the dry summer begins. Such plants die and wither away in the heat, but their seeds are safe on the warm ground till fall rains soak the earth and set them growing again. In the high mountains a thick blanket of snow covers the sleeping seeds till May or June, and then sunshine wakes them once more.

No doubt you have seen many of our shrubs or tall bush-plants in your vacations. Do you remember the sweet creamy white azaleas and the buckeyes that grow along the creeks in the redwoods? And the feathery blue blossoms of the wild lilac crowding in close thickets up the hillsides? One of our shrubs is a holiday visitor, the Christmas-berry, whose bright-red clusters trim your house at that gay, happy season. The manzanita is another pretty bush, with pink bells that ripen to small scarlet apples in the fall.

Usually, these and other shrubs cover the hillsides with a thick, matted tangle of stems and branches almost impossible to get through. This chaparral, as the Spanish called it, clothes the foot-hills and mountain sides with a close growth through which deer and bears alone can travel and make trails or runways. Great stretches of buckthorn in the north, and of sage-brush in the south, cover the wild lands, while in the sandy desert tall, prickly cactus, yucca, and mesquite grow with the sage-brush in the blazing sun.

IN A MISSION GARDEN.
Click photo to see full-sized.

Only a few of California's wild plants and flowers have been now called to your notice. But children have sharp eyes, and you will find many more to inquire about in your vacation days. Then the blackberries and thimble-berries will be ripe, and the pink salmon-berry in the redwoods. Perhaps you will look for and dig up the soaproot, that onion-like bulb of one of the lily family with which the Indians make a soapy lather to wash their clothes. Let us hope you will know and keep away from the "poison-oak," the low bush with pretty red leaves, for its leaves are apt to make your skin swell up and blister wherever they touch you.

What a long and pleasant story might be told you of our state's real gardens! Perhaps your teacher will give you an hour to talk about your home gardens, and to see how much you can tell about them. You may have flowers the year round, if you live on the coast, or in the warm valleys where no Jack Frost comes with his icy breath to kill the tender plants. In such genial climates roses and geraniums bloom all year, and only rest when the gardener cuts them back; and most of the shrubs and trees in parks and gardens are always fresh and green.

Florists who raise flowers to sell find that here they can grow the choicest and finest carnations, roses, and all the garden blossoms you know so well. Many of these florists deal only in flower-seeds, and bulbs or roots of the lilies to send to the Eastern states or abroad, where people greatly prize California flowers.

PALMS OVER 100 YEARS OLD
AT LOS ANGELES.
Click photo to see full-sized.

Plants and trees from all parts of the world thrive here, also. You have seen the palms, the tall sword-palm with its great spike of snowy bloom in the spring, the fan-palm whose dried and trimmed leaves are really used for fans, and, perhaps, the date-palm. This tree was planted round the Missions by the Padres, and some, more than a hundred years old, are still standing at the San Gabriel Mission. These, and the magnolia with its large creamy blossoms, as well as the graceful pepper-tree, are natives of warm, southern lands, while the eucalyptus, or gum-tree, was brought here from Australia.

Look round, children, as you walk to and from school, or in the park, and try to know and name the green things growing there, the flowers and plants sent to make our world a pleasant place to live in.

THE BIG TREES AND LUMBERING

The largest trees in the world are those forest giants of California which grow on the western slopes of the Sierra Nevadas, and nowhere else on the globe. People carelessly call these grand trees "redwoods" or "big trees," but their family name is Sequoia, an Indian chief's name. When the trees were first discovered, in 1853, accounts of their height and size were sent to England. Supposing this giant to be a new tree, it was there christened *Wellingtonia*, and also *gigantea* for its immense measurements. While Americans were trying to have it called *Washingtonia*, a famous Frenchman who knew all about trees decided that the specimen sent him was certainly a sequoia, as named by a German professor some six years before this time. So the tree was called *sequoia gigantea* and quietly went on growing, unmindful of the four nations who had quarrelled over its christening. Why, indeed, should it bother its lofty head with the chatter of people whose countries were unknown when this mighty tree was full grown? For these sequoias are the oldest of living objects and have probably been growing for four thousand years. How do we know this? Well, when a fallen trunk is sawed across, one can see rings in the wood, and it is thought that each ring is a year's growth. John Muir counted over four thousand of these annual rings on the stump of one of the Kings River trees.

These fine old trees grow in groves, and of the nine or ten groves the Calaveras and Mariposa are the best known. The Calaveras group of nearly a hundred mighty trees was the first one discovered, and four trees here are over three hundred feet high. The fallen "Father of the Forest" must have been much higher, for it measures a hundred feet round its trunk at the root end. A man can ride on horseback for two hundred feet through its hollow trunk as it lies on the ground. Many of the standing trees hollowed out by fires are large enough, used as cabins, to live in.

"WAWONA"
(28 feet in diameter).
Click photo to see full-sized.

THE GRIZZLY GIANT
(33 feet in diameter).
Click photo to see full-sized.

The Mariposa grove of Big Trees, being not far from Yosemite Valley, is the best known, as thousands of tourists visit both places. There is a big tree at Mariposa for every day in the year, and two very wonderful ones, the Grizzly Giant and Wawona. Stage-coaches drive into the grove through the tree Wawona, which was bored and burned out so as to make an opening ten by twelve feet. A wall of wood ten feet thick on each side of this opening supports the living tree. The great Grizzly Giant towers a hundred feet without a branch, and twice that height above the first immense branches that are six feet through. This was, no doubt, an old tree when Columbus discovered America, yet it is alive and green and still growing.

The largest tree in the world is the General Sherman, in Sequoia National Park, and it is thirty-five feet in diameter. This means that the stump of the tree, if smoothed off, would make a floor on which thirty people might dance, or your whole class be seated. You can scarcely imagine what a mighty column such a tree is, with its rich red-brown bark, fluted like a column, too, and with its crown of feathery green branches and foliage. The bark is a foot or two thick. The trees are evergreens, and conifers, or cone-bearers. Sequoia cones are two or three inches long and full of small seeds. The Douglas squirrel gets most of these seeds, but there are still seedlings and saplings or young trees enough to keep the race alive in most of the groves.

These groves of wonderful and rare trees are protected as National Parks in the Sequoia and Grant groves, and Mariposa belongs to the state. It is against the law to cut the trees in those groves. Their worst enemy is fire, and a troop of cavalry is sent every year to guard them, and to keep out the sheep-herders, whose flocks would destroy the underbrush and young trees. But, unfortunately, lumbermen have put up mills near the Fresno and Kings River groups, and, wasting more than they use, are destroying magnificent trees thousands of years old in order to make shingles. When nature has taken such good care of this rare and wonderful tree, the Sierra Giant, men should try to preserve the groves unharmed in all their beauty.

Another *sequoia* grows in great forests along the Coast Range from Santa Cruz to the northern state-line, and beyond into Oregon. This is the *sequoia sempervirens*, the Latin name meaning always green. Redwood is its common name, and the lumber for our frame or wooden houses is cut from this tree. Millions of feet of this redwood lumber are shipped from the northern counties of the state every year, up to Alaska or down to Central and South America. It is also sent far across the Pacific to the Hawaiian and Philippine islands and to China and Australia.

While the *sequoia gigantea* delights in a clear sky and hot sunshine, its brother, the *sempervirens*, prefers a cool sea-coast climate, offering frequent baths of fog. There is also a difference in the size of these trees; the redwood is often three hundred feet high, but is less in girth than its relative in the Sierras. There is not much underbrush and little sunshine in the cool, green redwood forests, each tree rising tall and stately for a hundred feet without branches, while the green tops seem almost to touch the sky as one looks up. Through the woods one hears the blue jay scream and chatter, and the tap, tap of the woodpecker as he drills holes in the bark to fill with acorns for his winter store.

When the lumberman looks at these beautiful forests, he sees only many logs containing many thousand feet of lumber, which he must get out the easiest and cheapest way. He only chooses the finest and largest trunks, and there is great waste in cutting these. The men begin to saw the tree some eight or ten feet from the ground, and soon it trembles and falls with a mighty crash, often snapping off other trees in its way to the ground. After all the selected trees have fallen, fires are started to burn off the branches and underbrush so that the men can work easier. This fire only chars the outside bark of the big, green logs, but it kills all the young saplings, and leaves the once beautiful forest a waste of blackened logs and gray ashes. When the fire burns itself out, the logs are usually sawed with a cross-cut saw into sixteen-foot lengths, since in that form they are easy to handle. Then oxen or horses haul them out; or sometimes a wire cable is fastened to them by iron "dogs," or stakes, and a little stationary engine pulls them away to the siding at the railroad track. Here they are rolled on flat-cars, fastened with a big iron chain around the four or six logs on the car, and taken on the logging train to the mill-pond. They lie soaking in the water until drawn up to the keen saws of the sawmill that cut and slice the wood like cheese. The bark and outside is carved off as you would cut the crust off bread, and then sharp, circular saws cut boards and planks till the log is used up, and the log-carriage lifts another to its place. As the shining steel bites into the wood the noise almost deafens you and the mill shakes with the thunder of log-carriage and feeders. Useless ends, slabs, and refuse are burnt in the sawdust pit, where the fires never go out. Very much of the tree is wasted and all the limbs. The redwood tree has so much life and strength, however, that it sends up bright green sprouts around the burnt stump, and standing trees charred outside to the tops will have new branches the next season. In the older forests tall young trees are often seen growing in a ring round an empty spot, the long-dead stump having rotted away.

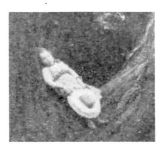

BIG TREES AT FELTON,
SANTA CRUZ CO.
Click photo to see full-sized.

Near Santa Cruz is a grove of large and beautiful redwoods, many of the trees being over three hundred feet high and from forty to sixty-five feet around the base of the trunk. The Giant is the largest, and three other immense ones are named for Generals Grant, Sherman, and Fremont. In

1846 General Fremont found this grove, and camped, on a rainy winter night, in the hollow trunk of the tree bearing his name. Here is also seen a group of eleven very tall trees growing in a circle around an old stump.

In the Sierras, both in the *sequoia* groves and forests above the Big-Tree region, are very large sugar-pines, red firs, and yellow-pine trees, all of which make excellent lumber. Great forests of these trees, with cedars almost as large as the redwoods, are in the northern counties also. You may have seen sugar-pine cones which are over a foot long, the largest of all found, while redwood cones are the smallest. Another great tree is the Douglas spruce, the king of spruce trees, growing in both Sierra Nevada and Coast ranges.

The California laurel, or bay tree, with its beautiful, shining green leaves, and the madroño, the slender, red-barked tree on the hillsides you must have noticed in your trips to the country, as well as our fine valley and mountain oaks. Try to learn the kinds of trees and study their leaves, blossoms, and fruit, and you will find every one a friend well worth knowing. Then you will wish to save them from fire and the lumberman's axe, especially the rare and old *sequoias*.

OUR BIRDS

More than three hundred kinds of these dear feathered friends and visitors live in California. Along the sea-shore, in the great valleys and the mountain-forests and meadows, even in the dry, hot desert, the birds, our shy and merry neighbors, are at home. In many parts of the state they find sunshine and green trees the year round, and food always at hand. Yet sparrows, robins, and woodpeckers will stay in the snowed-in groves of the Sierras all winter, contentedly chirping or singing in spite of the bitter cold.

If you know these wanderers of wood and field, these birds of sea and shore, and their interesting habits, you will wish to protect them from stone or gun, and their nests from the egg collector. You will listen to the lark and linnet, and be glad that the happy songster trilling such sweet notes is free to fly where he wishes, and is not pining in a cage. And you, little girl, will not encourage the destruction of these pretty creatures by wearing a sea-gull or part of some dead bird on your hat.

To become better acquainted with birds, let us call them before us by classes, beginning with our sea-birds and those round the bays and on the coast. Some of these not only swim but dive in the salt waters, and to this class of divers belong the grebe, loon, murre, and puffin. They dive at the flash of a gun, and after what seems a long time, come up far away from the spot the hunter aimed at. These birds usually nest on bare, rocky cliffs near the ocean, or on islands like the Farallones, and their large green eggs hatch out nestlings that are ugly and awkward and helpless on land. But they ride the great ocean-breakers, or dive into their clear depths easily and gracefully; and as they live upon fish or small sea-creatures, the divers only seek land to roost at night and to raise their young.

Next come the gulls, who belong to a class known as "long-winged swimmers." They have strong wings and fly great distances, and with their webbed feet swim well, too. Most of the sea-gulls are white with a gray coat on their backs, but they look snowy-white as they fly. You may see them walking about the wharves, or perching on roofs and piles watching for food, and seeming very tame as they pick up bits of bread or the refuse floating in the water. They follow steamers for miles, scarcely moving their wings as they float in the air; and if you throw a cracker from the deck, some gull will make a swift swoop and snatch it before the cracker reaches the water.

Far out on the Pacific the albatross sails proudly on his broad wings, and cares nothing for high winds or storms. He rests and sleeps on the billows at night with his little companions, the stormy petrels. He is the largest and strongest of our birds of flight, the very king of the sea. The stormy petrels are not much larger than a swallow. Sailors call them. "Mother Carey's chickens," and are sure a storm is coming up when petrels follow the ship. The albatross, petrel, and a gull-like bird called a shearwater belong to the "tube-nosed swimmers," on account of their curious long beaks.

Along the coast, and wading in the shallow waters around the bays, are some strange birds known as pelicans and shags. They are good fishers, and drive the darting, finny fellows before them as they wade in the water till they can see and gobble them up. Most waders have under their beaks a skin-pocket deep enough to hold a fish while carrying it to their nestlings, or making ready to swallow it. All of these sea-birds raise their young as far from the shore and from hunters as possible. Great flocks of them roost on islands fifteen or twenty miles out in the ocean, and fly into the bays every morning.

Wild ducks, geese, the herons, mud-hens, sandpipers, and curlews are marsh and shore birds that feed and wade in the shallow salt water, and nest on the banks or, like the heron, in trees near the bay. The heron is a frog-catcher, and he will stand very still on his long legs and patiently wait till the frog, thinking him gone, swims near. Then one dart of the long bill captures froggy, and the heron waits for another. You know the red-head, green mallard, canvas-back, and small teal ducks, no doubt, and have seen the flocks of wild geese flying and calling in the sky, or standing like patches of snow as they feed in the marshes or grain-fields.

Down on the mud-flats at low tide you see birds called rails, and also "kill-dee" plovers. The shoveller ducks are there, too fishing up with broad, flat beaks little crabs and such creatures as are in the mud, straining out mud and water, but swallowing the rest. All these birds are "waders" and delight in mud and cold salt water. They are usually quiet, or make only strange, shrill cries.

In the sunny fields and woods we shall find many of the land-birds, and first comes a family whose habits are so like those of chickens that they are called "scratchers." These birds depend for food upon seeds and bugs or worms they scratch out of the ground. Up in the Sierra sugar-pines and fir-woods lives the largest of these "scratchers," the brown grouse. He is a shy creature, rising out of his feeding-ground with a great whirring of wings and out of sight before the hunter can fire at him. His peculiar cry, or "drumming," as it is called, sounds through the woods like tapping hard on a hollow log. His equally shy neighbor is the mountain-quail, while through the farming lands and all along the hillsides the valley—quail are plenty. Perhaps you have seen a happy family of these speckled brown birds. Papa quail has a black crest on his head, and he calls "Look right here" from the wrong side of the road to fool you, while Mamma and her little, cunning chicks scatter like flying brown leaves in the brush. After the danger is past, you hear her low call to bring them round her again. In the desert and sage-brush part of the state the sage-hen, another "scratcher," runs swiftly through the thickets, but many are caught and brought in by the Indians.

Our birds of prey are eagles, vultures, hawks, owls, and the turkey-buzzards, those big black scavengers that hang in the air. In circles high above woods and fields some of these birds of prey sweep on broad wings, searching with keen sight for their food in some dead animal far below. The California condor, a great black vulture-like bird, is almost extinct, and is only found in the highest mountains. It is very large of wing, and strong enough, it is said, to carry off a sheep. Both golden and bald eagles nest in tall trees in the wildest parts of the state. The chicken-hawk, whose swift sailing over the poultry-yard calls out loud squawking from the frightened hens, you have often seen, and the wise-looking brown owls, too. A small burrowing owl lives in the squirrel holes, and you may catch him easily in the daytime, when he cannot see.

The road-runner is of the cuckoo family of birds. It seldom flies, but runs swiftly along the roads, or in the desert, and is said to kill rattlesnakes by placing a ring of thorny cactus leaves around the snake as it lies asleep. The rattler is then pecked to death, since it cannot get out of its prickly cage. This fowl is like a slender brown hen in size.

In the redwoods you hear the tap, tap, of the "carpenter" woodpecker, with his black coat and gay red cap. He drills holes in the bark of a tree with his strong beak and then fits an acorn neatly into each safe little storehouse. It is thought that worms and grubs fatten while living in these acorns, so that the woodpecker always has a meal ready in the winter when the ground is wet, or the squirrels have carried off the acorns under the trees.

Humming-birds, or "hummers," as the boys call them, are plenty in city and country and so fearless that they will take a bath in the spray of the garden-hose, or dart their long bills in the fuchsias almost within your reach. The bill shields a double tongue, which gets not only honey, but small insects from the flower or off the leaves. The humming-bird's tiny nest is a soft, round basket, not much bigger than half a walnut-shell, and holding two eggs, which are like small-white beans. Bits of moss and gray cobwebs are woven in this nest till it looks like the branch itself; and here the little mother in her plain brown dress hatches out and feeds the baby "hummers." Her husband has glistening ruby feathers at his throat and green spots on his head and back that glow in the sun like jewels.

The highest class of birds is the "perchers," and many friends of yours belong to this. There are two families, however, of perchers, those that call and the song-birds. Calling over and over their peculiar note, the pewees, flycatchers, and king-birds, fly through the forests. The crow and blue jay belong to the singers, you will be surprised to hear. And what a crowd of these song-birds there are trilling and warbling in the sunshine! Have you ever watched the meadow-lark singing as he sits on guard on the fence, while the rest of his brown-coated yellow-vested flock run along the field picking up seeds and insects?

BABY YELLOW WARBLERS.
From photographs
by Elizabeth Grinnell.
Click photo to see full-sized.

Then there are the linnets, or "redheads," who sing their sweet, merry tunes all summer, and if they do take a cherry or two the farmer should not grumble. They destroy many bugs and caterpillars and eat weed-seeds that might trouble the fruit-grower more than the missing cherries. The yellow warbler, sometimes called the wild canary, flits through bush and tree and trills its gay notes in town and country. Song-sparrows, thrushes, and bluebirds warble far and near, while the red-winged blackbird makes music in wet, swampy places. The robin, who comes to city gardens in the winter, has a summer home in the mountains or redwoods. There, too, the saucy jay screams and chatters, and flashes his blue wings as he flies, scolding all the time.

In Southern California, among the orange groves or in gardens, the mocking-bird trills in sweet, liquid notes his wonderful song. He mimics, too, many sounds he hears, and sometimes when caged will whistle tunes or say words. The mocker can crow or cackle like the chickens, or mew like the cat. Then he will whistle clear and loud till dogs or boys answer his call. When they find themselves fooled, it is said, he mimics a laugh.

YOUNG TOWHEE.
Click photo to see full-sized.

From April to July the birds are busy, nesting, feeding their families, or teaching them to fly. Many eggs never hatch, and some are destroyed by wild animals. Boys often rob a whole nest to have one little blown egg in their collections. Then again the mother is killed and her brood starves to death. When the parent birds are teaching the nestlings to fly, cats also catch the little ones. So you see the poor feathered things have many enemies.

Let us try to protect the birds, and to let them live happy lives in freedom. Each one will thank you, either with sweet songs or with being a beautiful thing to see on land or ocean.

OUR WILD ANIMALS

Once upon a time, when the Spanish owned this state and called it their province of Alta California, there were great herds of antelope feeding on the grassy plains, and at every little stream elk and deer and big grizzly bears came down to drink. No fences had been built, and the wild animals had never heard a rifle-shot. Free and fearless they ranged valley and hillside, or made their dens in the thick brush, or "chaparral," as the Spanish called it.

Indian hunters watched the paths over which these wild creatures travelled to water, and killed deer and antelope with their arrows. But these hunters were afraid of grizzly bears, for an arrow in Mr. Bear's thick hide only made him cross, and with one hug, or even a light blow from his paw, he could cripple the poor Indian. So in those early days the old bears came year after year, and carried off sheep and cattle. The simple folks did not even try to kill them. Indeed, many of the red men believed that very bad Indians were punished by being turned into grizzly bears when they died, and they would not hurt their brothers, they said.

When Father Serra's Mission people were starving at Monterey, the Padre learned that at a place called Bear Valley near by, there were many grizzlies which the Indians would not kill. He sent Spanish soldiers there, and they shot so many bears that the hungry Mission family had meat enough to last till a ship came from Mexico with supplies.

Of all flesh-eating animals this grizzly bear is the largest and strongest. He can knock down a bull with his great paws, or kill and carry off a horse. He can live on wild berries and acorns with grass and roots he digs out of the ground, yet fresh meat suits him best, and he prefers a calf, which he holds as a cat does a mouse.

Nothing but stock was raised in California in those days so long ago, and cattle were counted by the thousands and sheep by tens of thousands. Then the grizzly and cinnamon, or brown, bear feasted all the time on stray calves and yearlings. Every spring and fall the cattle, which had roamed almost wild in the pastures, were "rounded up" by the cowboys, or vaqueros. After the work of picking out each ranchero's stock and branding the young cattle was over, the vaqueros thought it fine fun to lasso a bear,—some old fellow, perhaps, who had been helping himself to the calves. It is told that one big cinnamon bear, while quietly feeding on acorns, looked up to find three or four cow-boys on their ponies in a circle around him. They spurred the trembling ponies as close to him as they dared, and yelled at the tops of their voices. The great brute sat up on his haunches and faced them, growling and snarling. One vaquero sent his rope flying through the air, and the loop settled over a big, hairy fore paw. Then the bear dropped on all fours and made a jump at the pony, which got out of his reach. Another Mexican threw a lasso and caught the bear's hind foot; and as he sat up again a third noose dropped over the other fore paw. Then the poor trapped creature, growling, snarling, and rolling over and over, began a tug of war with the lariats and the ponies. Once a rope broke, and horse and rider tumbled in front of the bear. He made a quick, savage jump, but was pulled back by the other ropes. Then Mr. Bear sat up straight and tugged so hard that another lariat broke and sent the saddle and rider over the pony's head. With one sweep of his paw the bear smashed the saddle, but the cowboy saved himself by running to an oak tree. At last Mr. Bear was getting the best of the fight so plainly, and had pulled the frightened ponies so near him, that the man who was thrown off ended the poor animal's struggles with a rifle-ball.

A Chinese sheep-herder tells this funny story about a bear: "Me lun out, see what matta; me see sheep all bely much scared, bely much lun, bely much jump. Big black bear jump over fence, come light for me. Me so flighten me know nothin', then me scleam e-e-e-e so loud, and lun at bear till bear get scared too and lun away."

A few grizzlies are still found in the Sierras, and black and brown bears are often seen with their playful little cubs. The small fellows are easily tamed and may be taught many tricks. They will live contentedly in a bear-pit, or even if chained up, and as most of you know, they like peanuts and popcorn well enough to beg for them.

The panther, or mountain-lion, is another large flesh-eating animal which makes his home in the thick woods conveniently neighboring the farmers' corrals and pastures. Not long ago a boy in Marin County, who was sent to look after some ponies, saw a big yellow dog, as he thought, "worrying" one of the colts. When he came nearer he found it was a wicked-looking, catlike creature, and knew it must be a California lion. He had nothing with him but a heavy whip. The panther left the wounded colt and crouched ready to spring at the boy, but he was on the alert and struck it a terrible blow across the eyes with his whip, and then another and another. Half-blinded and whining with pain, the panther turned tail and ran away, while the boy's pony, trembling and snorting with fright, galloped home with his brave rider.

In one of the mountain counties a woman, hearing her chickens squawking one day at noon, ran out to find what seemed a big dog among them with a hen in his mouth. She rushed straight at him with a broom, when the animal turned. She found it was a great panther, who snarled and made ready to spring at her. As she screamed and started to run away, her foot slipped on a steep and muddy place, and she slid down the little hill right into the panther's face. He was so frightened that he jumped the fence and hurried to the woods.

This great yellow cat is both savage and cowardly, and he has been known to follow a man walking through the woods, all day, yet he sneaked out of sight at every loud call the man gave. He chases deer and gets many small and helpless fawns, hunters say.

Fur-hunting was once a profitable business for the Indians, who were clothed in bear and panther skins when the first white men came to California, and had many furs to trade or sell. The Indians trapped otters, beavers, and minks, and the squaws tanned the deer-hides to make buckskin shirts or leggings. Hunters and trappers still bring in these wild animals' furry coats after trips to the high mountains or untravelled woods, where the shy creatures try to live and be safe from their enemies.

CALIFORNIA RED DEER.
From a photograph by
George V. Robinson.
Click photo to see full-sized.

In early days herds of a very large deer, called elk, fed on the wild oats and grass. These elk had wide, branching horns measuring three or four feet from tip to tip. Only a few of them now survive in the redwood forests in the northern counties. There were plenty of them once where San Francisco now stands. Dana in his book called "Two Years Before the Mast," tells us that when his ship dropped anchor off the little village of Yerba Buena about sixty-seven years ago, he saw hundreds of red deer and elk with their branching antlers. They were running about on the hills, or standing still to look at the ship until the noise frightened them off. At that time the whole country was covered with thick trees and bushes where the wolf and coyote prowled, and the grizzly bear's track was seen everywhere.

There are plenty of deer in the redwoods now, and in the high Sierras are black-tailed and large mule-deer. In the woods round Mount Tamalpais timid red deer live, too. In winter, when it is cold and snowy in the northern counties of our state, these deer often come into the farmer's barnyard to nibble at the hay.

There are still left in the mountains among the pines and snowy cliffs many mountain-sheep. These curious big-horned animals resemble both the elk and the sheep, and it is said they can jump from a high rock and land far below on their feet or heavy, twisted horns without being hurt in the least.

Of all the great herds of graceful, fast-running antelope, once the most plentiful of our wild animals, only a very few can now be found on the eastern slopes of the Sierras.

But Master Coyote, who might well be spared, so cruel and cowardly is he, still sneaks up and down the whole state, and his quick sharp bark gives notice that the rascal is ready to steal a chicken or a lamb if it is not protected. With his bushy tail and large head he is half fox and half wolf in appearance, and mean enough in habits to be both. He can outrun a dog and even a deer, and though he catches jack-rabbits and the Molly Cottontail usually for food, he would help his brother, the wolf, to kill a poor harmless sheep.

This gray wolf is a savage creature and hides in the thick forests by day, slinking out at night to the nearest sheep corral or turkey-pen if he can find one unwatched by some faithful dog. His friend and neighbor, the fox, likes fat geese and chickens as well as birds, squirrels, and wood-rats. The queer raccoon lives in the redwoods and is often caught and kept in a cage or chained for a pet.

Wildcats, both gray and yellow, are found in the thickly timbered parts of California, and the badger makes his home in the mountain cañons or pine woods. There, too, the curious porcupine dwells. He is covered with grayish white quills, which bristle out when he is angry or frightened. No old dog will touch this animal, for he knows better than to get a mouthful of sharp toothpicks by biting Mr. Porcupine, who is like a round pincushion with the pins pointing out. A dog who has never seen this prickly ball will dab at it, and have a sore paw to nurse for weeks after.

Two or three kinds of tree-squirrels live in the pines and redwoods, the Douglas squirrel being well known in the mountains. The ground squirrel, or chipmunk, digs holes in the ground, where he hides his winter's store of grain and nuts.

Three of our smaller wild animals are very common and very troublesome to the farmer. The skunk, which looks like a pretty black and white kitten with a bushy tail, and also the weasel, destroy all the chickens and eggs they can reach, and they are so cunning that it is hard to keep them out of the hen-house. That little pest, the gopher, we are all well acquainted with, since he gnaws the pinks and roses off at their roots in your city garden while his large family of brothers and sisters kill the farmer's fruit-trees and vines. The gopher digs long tunnels under ground, making storerooms here and there in these passages, which he fills with grass, roots, and seeds. In each cheek he has a pouch, or pocket, large enough to hold nearly a handful of grain, so the little rascal carries his stores very easily. The traps and poison by which the farmer is always trying to make way with him, he is sly enough to let alone. His greatest foe is the cat, which watches patiently at the hole where the destructive little fellow is digging and usually catches him. A mother cat will sometimes bring in two or three gophers a day to her kittens.

IN SALT WATER AND FRESH

Tom and Retta Ransom were two of the happiest children in the state, I believe, when told that their summer vacation was to be spent at Catalina Island. To see the wonderful fish that swim in those warm, Southern waters, to watch them through the glass-bottomed boat, to dip out funny sea-flowers with a net, or catch the pretty kingfish and perhaps a "yellowtail,"—why, they could talk of nothing else!

How they skipped and danced and chattered about the trip! At last Mamma said, "Well, everything is packed and ready, and we go to-morrow." Then what fun it was to stand on the steamer's deck and sail "right out through the Golden Gate," as Retta said. The big green billows of the Pacific Ocean caught the boat as she crossed the outside bar and tossed salt spray almost into their faces. Little the children cared for the drops of water, for they were so glad to be off on their trip and to say good-by to San Francisco's summer fog and cold winds for a time.

SEAL ROCKS,
SAN FRANCISCO.
Click photo to see full-sized.

And there on Seal Rocks, near the Cliff House, were the seals, or rather sea-lions, clumsy creatures like black rubber sacks with fins, or flippers, and a head. Some were lying in the sun and others crawling up the steep, wet rocks. Those highest up were asleep and quiet, but most of them kept barking or growling as they tried to find a sunny place to bask in. Sometimes when frightened these sea-lions will pitch headlong from high rocks into the ocean and dive out of sight at once. Mrs. Ransom said she remembered seeing one that was kept for years in a salt-water tank, and that, although they seem so clumsy, this sea-lion jumped so quick that he caught a fish thrown to him before it touched the water. Once fur-seals were in great numbers off our coast, and lived on the rocks as these sea-lions now do. But Indians, or later on white hunters, killed them, or drove them up north where the crack of the rifle is not heard.

On to the south the steamer sailed through the foaming waters, and as Tom stood watching the white-capped waves go dancing by, he saw, two or three times, a black fin come up, and then another. At last a man said, "Look at the porpoises playing." Tom screamed with delight as they jumped and chased each other till their black, shiny backs were clear out of water. These fish are sometimes called sea-hogs and are five or six feet long. Either to get their food of small fish, or in play, they keep swimming and diving near the tops of the breakers. Fishermen catch them with a strong hook and use the thick, leathery skin for straps or strings, while they try oil out of their blubber or fat.

HUMPBACK WHALE
(57 feet long).
Click photo to see full-sized.

All that day and night the boat kept steadily on her way, and the next morning they were in Santa Barbara Channel. It was so pleasant sailing on this summer sea in the soft, warm sunshine that even the sea-sick ladies felt better and came on deck. Mamma agreed with the children that the steamer trip was much nicer than the hot, dusty cars. Just then some one called, "See the whale," and looking quick Tom and Retta saw what seemed a fountain of water rising high in the air about half a mile away. Soon another went up, and two or three more, for the gray hump-backed whales like this stretch of smooth bay. They are warm-blooded animals and not fish at all, so they must come to the top of the waves for air to breathe. The air and water spout out through "blow-holes" on top of the whale's head, and rise like steam in the colder air. The children's mother told them that the whale is the largest of all animals, and that it lives on little jellyfish. It swims with its great mouth wide open and catches all the tiny sea creatures in its path. A fringe of whalebone hangs down from the roof of the whale's mouth, and he strains the water out through this and swallows the fish. As the boat went on, the children said, "There she blows," as the sailors do when they see whales spouting in the distance.

Late that night the steamer got to San Pedro, and you may be sure Tom and Retta were up early the next morning. As they came off the boat, there was a crowd of people on the wharf who were pulling in "yellow-tail" as fast as they dropped their lines. This fine fish is a little like a big salmon, but with golden-yellow fins and tail. Its body is greenish gray, with spots of the prettiest rainbow colors, which grow brighter as the fish dies. These fish bite easily, but as soon as caught begin to rush back and forth, fighting and trying to snap the line.

The children here took a smaller steamer for the twenty-mile trip across to Catalina Island, and on the way over they saw a whole "school" of whales and a flight of flying-fishes. Yes, really and truly, these little fish fly or sail through the air, for their fins balance them like a parachute. They skim along ten or twelve feet above the waves, and then drop in the water to rest, taking another flight whenever their enemies, the porpoises, chase them.

How happy the children were to land at the little town of Avalon, and to know that they were to have a month at this beautiful place! They hurried down to the beach and their first choice of amusements was the glass-bottomed boat. These boats have "water-telescopes," which are only clear glass set in boxed-in places. The glass seems to make the ripples still, so that you can look down, down to the bottom of the ocean, twenty or thirty feet below you.

The boatman rowed the children out in the bay, where the water, now green, now blue, was always clear as crystal. On the rocks and sand at the bottom starfish and crabs crawled slowly along or clung to some stone. The purple sea-urchins, queer round-shelled creatures covered with thorny spines, crowded together, and the ugly toad-fish hid in the green and brown seaweeds. Blue, purple, and rainbow-colored jellyfish floated on top of the waters, while gold perch with red and green sunfish swam through the seaweed "like parrots in some hot country's woods," Retta thought. In the shallow places on the rocks those curious sea-flowers, the anemones, looked like pink or green cactus blossoms. The children never tired of the water-telescope in all their stay at the island.

BLACK SEA BASS.
Click photo to see full-sized.

LEAPING   TUNA.
Click photo to see full-sized.

At night the warm ocean waters seemed on fire, since they are full of very tiny, soft-bodied creatures, each of which gives out a faint, glowing light. Every day the fishermen brought in new and strange fishes. The black sea-bass, heavier than the fisherman himself and longer than he was tall, were wonderful, and they could hardly believe that such big fish were caught with a rod and line.

But the leaping tuna pleased Tom the most, since he thought it such fun to watch them jump into the air like silver arrows after the flying-fish. Not so large as the black bass, the tunas are strong enough to tow a boat along when running with a hook. One will drag a heavy launch through the water as if a tug had hold of it, and will fight for hours, rushing and plunging till tired out. Then the fisherman pulls him up to the boat and ends his struggles.

Tom and Retta were fond of watching the curious fish and sea-plants in the glass aquarium tanks on shore also, but their happiest time was when they gathered shells on the beach. They never found out the names of more than those of the limpet, turban, and scallop, though they picked up baskets full of tiny pink and white beauties, all frail and of many kinds. These shells were once the homes of sea mollusks, as such soft, fleshy creatures are called. But to Tom and Retta the shells were only pretty playthings, to be doll's dishes, or cups, or pincushions, perhaps.

One morning some fishermen saw a shark, and no one dared to go in bathing for a few days. This great, savage, "man-eater" shark does not often come north of the Gulf of California. Sometimes small ones are caught with a hook and line off Catalina Island, and Tom was always glad to see such sea-tigers destroyed.

Of course the children did not want to go home, till at last Mrs. Ransom explained to them that in the ocean and bay near San Francisco there were odd fish and strange animals too. And so it turned out, for in a day's fishing over at Sausalito Tom caught many silver smelt and tomcod, with flat, ugly flounders, and a red, big-eyed rock-cod. The frightened boy almost fell out of the boat, too, when he pulled in a large sting-ray, or "stingaree," as the boatman called it. This queer three-sided fish, with a sharp, bony sting in its back, flopped round till the man cut the hook out, knocked its head till it was no longer able to bite, and threw it overboard. These rays have to be fenced out of the oyster-beds along the bay, since they have big mouths full of such strong teeth that they crush an oyster, shell and all, and destroy every one they can reach.

Oysters are grown in great quantities in the oyster-beds along the bay shore. The largest size, which are called "transplanted," are brought from the East as very small or baby oysters and dropped into shallow water, where they cling to rocks or brush-piles till grown.

Tom also caught a perch, and clinging to it as he drew in his line was a large, hard-shelled, long-clawed crab. Tom put the crab in the basket, knowing well what delicious white meat was in the fellow's legs and back.

Clams that burrow deep in the mud and may be found at low tide, by digging where their tell-tale bubble of air arises, and the odd shrimps, so good to eat, the children already knew about. Chinese fishermen catch shrimps in nets, dry them on the hillsides, and send both dry meat and shells to China. They dry the meat of the abalone also, and use the beautiful shells, which you have no doubt seen, for carving into curios, or making into jewellery.

A salt-water creature very destructive to shipping and the wharves is the teredo, or ship-worm. This brown inch-long worm lives in wood that is always under water, such as the bottoms of ships and the round piles you see at the wharves. He hollows or bores out winding tunnels in the wood with the sharp edge of his shell until the piles crumble to pieces. This small animal would finally destroy the largest wooden ship if sheets of copper were not put on the sides and keel to protect it.

TROUT FROM LAKE TAHOE.
Click photo to see full-sized.

When Retta saw Tom's basket of fish she said, "Well, I think the fresh-water fishes much prettier. I am sure the rainbow and Dolly Varden trout with their bright-colored spots, which we saw up in the Truckee River and the mountain lakes last summer, were better to look at and to eat than these sea monsters." Tom laughed and said, "Oh, that was because you helped to catch some of those. Do you remember the big black-spotted trout we saw in Lake Tahoe? And the little speckled fellows we caught in that clear creek in the redwoods, and how we wrapped them in wet paper and cooked them at our camp-fire? I wish we could go up to the McCloud River, though, and see the baby trout in the fish hatchery there."

So their mother told them that the tiny trout eggs were kept in troughs with clear, cold water running over them till they hatched out. Then the little things, not half as long as a pin, were placed in large tin cans and sent to stock brooks and lakes, and in a year or so they grew big enough to catch.

The most valuable of our food-fishes is the salmon, a large silvery-sided salt-water fish that takes fresh-water journeys too. For they swim up the rivers every year to lay their eggs in the clear, cold streams, knowing, perhaps, that the salmon-fry, as the young are called, will have fewer enemies away from the ocean. The salmon go over a hundred miles up to the McCloud River to spawn, and will jump or leap up small falls or rapids in their way.

Indians spear many of them, but a number go back to the ocean again. Thousands and thousands of ocean salmon are caught along the northern coast and taken to the canneries. There the fish are put into cans and cooked, and when sealed up are sent all over the world. California salmon is eaten from Iceland to India, and its preparation and sale give employment to many people.

ABOUT CALIFORNIA'S INDIANS

When the Spanish and English first landed on this part of the New World's coast, they found the Indians who dwelt inland almost naked, and living like wild animals on roots and seeds and acorns. The tribes along the seashore, however, were good hunters and fishermen, and those Indians along the Santa Barbara Channel and the islands near by were a tall, fine-looking people, and the most intelligent of the race. They had large houses and canoes, and clothed themselves in sealskins.

The Indians Drake saw near Point Reyes had fur coats, or cloaks, but no other clothes. They brought him presents of shell money or wampum, and of feather head-dresses and baskets. With their bows and arrows they killed fish or deer or squirrels, and being very strong ran swiftly after game. They seemed gentle and peaceable with the white men and each other, and were sorry to have Drake sail away.

In later years the Indians who lived here when the Mission Padres came were stupid and brutish, because they knew nothing better. They were lazy, dirty, and at first would not work. But the patient Padres taught them to raise grain and fruit, to build their fine churches, to weave cloth and blankets, and to tan leather for shoes, saddles, or harness. But although the Indians learned to be good workmen, they liked idleness, dancing, and feasting much better, and when the Missions were given up the Indians soon went back to their former habits.

There were no distinct tribes among these Indians, and they had no laws. Nor was there a king or chief over many natives. They lived in small villages or rancherias, each having a name and ruled by a captain. Each rancheria had its special place to hunt or fish, and had to fight its own battles with the other families of Indians.

INDIAN WOMAN
WITH PAPPOOSE.
Click photo to see full-sized.

The men did nothing but hunt and fish, or make bows, stone arrow-heads, nets and traps for game. The women not only had to gather grass seeds, acorns, and nuts or berries, but they had to do all the field-work and carry the heavy burdens, usually with a baby strapped in its basket above the load. In preparing food for cooking, these mahalas, or squaws, put seed or acorns in a stone mortar and pounded them to coarse meal or paste. Sometimes a grass-woven basket was filled with water, and hot stones were thrown in till the water began to boil. Then acorn or seed meal was put in and cooked into mush. This meal, or that from wild oats, was also mixed into a dough and baked on hot stones into bread. Game or fish was eaten raw, or broiled a little on the coals of the camp-fire.

The Indians got many deer, and one way of hunting them was to put the head and hide of a deer over the hunter's head. The make-believe then crept along in the high grass till near enough to the quietly feeding animals to put an arrow through one or more. All the streams were full of fish then, and salmon swarmed in rivers that ran to the ocean. These salmon the Indians speared or shot with arrows. They also built runways or fish-weirs and made them so that the fish would become crowded into a narrow passage, and could easily be dipped out with nets or baskets.

When the Americans came here they called these Indians "Diggers," because they lived on what they could dig or root out of the ground. They were very fond of grasshoppers, and ate them either dried or raw, or made into a soup with acorn or nut-meal. Fat grubworms and the flesh of any animal found dead was a great treat. If a whale or sea-lion was washed ashore on the beach, the Indians gathered round it for a feast, and soon left only the bones.

But they had no idea of saving food, so they fattened when there was plenty, and starved when dry years made the acorns or nuts scarce. Having no salt, they did not try to dry or smoke the meat of deer or other wild animals. Nor did they at first lay up nuts and seeds, as even the squirrels or woodpeckers do, for winter use. But wandering from place to place, they camped in the summer along the rivers, where fish was plenty and the wild oats gave them grain. In the fall they hunted pine-nuts and berries in the mountains, till snow drove them down into the valleys.

Each Indian town, or rancheria, had a name, and many of these names are still in use. At the north lived the Klamaths, Siskiyous, Shastas, and the savage Modocs, whose months of fighting in the lava beds caused the death of General Canby and many soldiers. The Pomo tribes of Lake county, Yrekas, Hoopas, and Ukiahs, are well known at the present day. Tehama, Colusa, Tuolumne, Yosemite, and other places recall the Indians who gave each its name. The San Diego Indians are still known as Diegueños and live on a reserve, or lands set aside for them.

Almost all the natives had Indian money, called wampum, which they made from abalone or clam-shells by cutting out round pieces like buttons or small, hollow beads. Little shells were also used, and the wampum was strung on grass or on deer sinews. The Pomos still make thousands of pieces of this money, and so many strings of it will buy whatever the buck, or Indian man, and his mahala, or squaw, wish to get.

General Bidwell, who came to California in 1841 and surveyed the land for many ranches, says of the Indians at that time:—

"They were almost as wild as deer, and wore no clothes at all except the women, who had tule aprons fastened to a belt round their waists. In the rough work of surveying among brush and briars I gave the men shoes, pantaloons, and shirts, which they would take off when work was done, carry home in their hands, and put on in time to go to work again. But they soon learned to sleep in their new things to save trouble, and would wear them day and night till a suit dropped to pieces. They were quick to do as the whites did, and when paid in calico and cloth Saturday night, by Monday they had on their new skirts or shirts all made up like ours. Yet every Indian would choose beads for his wages, and go almost naked and hungry till the next pay-day."

General Bidwell treated the Indians honestly and kindly, and in return they were his friends and helped him much to his advantage. In 1847 he settled on the great Rancho Chico, and part of his land he gave to the

Mechoopdas, as the Indian rancheria there was called. They worked to plant orchards and at all his farm-work, and he treated them so fairly that old men are still living on this ranch who as boys helped the general in his tree-planting and road-building. A whole village of these Mechoopdas live on the Bidwell place owning their houses, while Mrs. Bidwell is their best friend and helps them in sickness and trouble. The men work in the hop fields and fruit orchards, and the women make baskets.

INDIAN WOMAN
WITH BASKETS.
Click photo to see full-sized.

INDIAN BASKETS.
Click photo to see full-sized.

All the California Indians are basket-makers, and their work is so well done and so beautiful that it is much prized. The Pomos of Lake and Mendocino counties make especially fine baskets for every purpose. Indeed, the Indian papoose, or baby, is cradled in a basket on his mother's back; he drinks and eats from cup or bowl-shaped baskets, and the whole family sleep under a great wicker tent basket thatched with grass or tules. All Pomo baskets are woven on a frame of willow shoots, and in and out through this the mahala draws tough grasses or fine tree roots dyed in different colors, and after the pattern she chooses. Sometimes she works into the baskets the quail's crest, small red or yellow feathers from the woodpecker, green from the head of the mallard duck, or beads. She also hangs wampum or bits of abalone shell on the finest ones. The storage baskets are four or five feet high to hold grain or acorns, and the baskets to fit the back and carry a load are like half a cone in shape, with straps to hold the burden in place. Their smaller berry baskets hold just a quart. Some are water-tight and are used to cook mush in. Fish-traps and long narrow basket-traps for quail are also made out of this willow-work.

On the Bidwell ranch is an old Indian "temescal," or sweat-house. It is an underground hut, or cave dug out of a hillside, with a hole in the top for smoke to reach the air. The Indians used to build a big fire in this cave and then lie round it till dripping with sweat. A cold plunge into the creek near by finished the bath,—Turkish, we call it. Nowadays the Indians use this place for a meeting-room and for dances.

The older Indians still dance and rig out in all their finery of feathers and beads, though the young people are ashamed of their tribal customs and wish to be like the white folks. Some of their dances are named for a bird or animal, and the Indians must imitate by their dress and cries the animal chosen. In the bear dance the dancer crawls about the fire on all fours with a bear's skin about him. He wears a chain of oak-balls round his neck, and as he shakes his head these rattle like a bear's teeth snapping shut, while all the time he growls savagely. The feather-dancer, with a skirt and cap of eagles' feathers, will whirl on his toes like a top for hours, while the other Indians sing and the master of the dance shakes a large rattle.

The California Indians are slowly passing away, and though all over the state there are still rancherias, the land that was once their very own will soon know them no more.

THE STORY OF SAN FRANCISCO

The Mission and Presidio of San Francisco were founded in 1776 by Father Palou, and two little settlements grew up around the fort and at the church. The Presidio was built where it is now, and ships used to anchor in the bay in front of it, though the whalers usually went to Sausalito to get wood from the hills and to fill their water-casks at a large spring. From early Mission times the Spanish name of Yerba Buena was given to that part of San Francisco's peninsula between Black Point and Rincon Point. Ship-captains and sailors soon found out that the cove or bay east of Yerba Buena was the best and least windy place to anchor their vessels, and later on hundreds of ships found a safe harbor there. The name Yerba Buena, or good herb, was given on account of a little creeping vine with sweet-smelling leaves which covered the ground and is still found on the sand-dunes and Presidio hills.

For many years the small settlements made no progress, and the rest of the peninsula was covered with thick woods, where the grizzly bear, wolf, and coyote roamed, while deer were plenty at the Presidio. Then in 1835 Governor Figueroa, the Mexican ruler of California, directed that a new town should be started at Yerba Buena cove. The first street, called the "foundation-street," was laid out from Pine and Kearny streets, as they are called to-day, to North Beach. The first house was built by Captain Richardson on what is now Dupont Street, between Clay and Washington. The next year a trader named Jacob Leese built a store. It was finished on the Fourth of July, and in honor of the day he gave a feast and a fandango, or dance, at which the company danced that night and all the next day. This was the first Fourth celebrated in the place.

Two or three years later a new survey laid out streets between Broadway and California, Montgomery and Powell. A fresh-water lagoon, or lake, was near the present corner of Montgomery and Sacramento, and an Indian temescal, or sweat-house, beside it. The bay came up to Montgomery Street then, with five feet of water at Sansome, and mudflats to the east. During the gold excitement of '49, when hundreds of ships dropped anchor in the bay, many sailors deserted to go to the mines, and some of the old vessels were hauled in on these mud-flats and made into storehouses. All that part of the city east of Montgomery Street is filled or made ground, and when new buildings are to be started wooden piles or cement piers must go down to get a firm foundation.

Until 1846 only about thirty families lived at Yerba Buena. Then a shipload of Mormon emigrants arrived and pitched their tents in the sand-hills.

Samuel Brannan, their leader, printed the first newspaper, *The California Star*, in '47. That year also the first alcalde, or mayor, of the new town, Lieutenant Bartlett, appointed an engineer named O'Farrell to lay out more streets. He surveyed Market Street and mapped down blocks as far west on the sand-dunes as Taylor Street and to Rincon Point or South Beach. He gave the names of such well-known men as Kearny, Stockton, Larkin, Guerrero, and Geary to these streets. Mission Street was the road to the Mission Dolores, and about this time Bartlett ordered that the Presidio, the Mission, and Yerba Buena should be one town and should be called San Francisco.

Then came the gold fever, and nearly every one left town to go to the mines. Many people sold all they had to get money to buy mining tools and food enough to live on till they struck gold. Men started for the mines, leaving their houses and stores alone with no one to care for goods or furniture.

But news of the finding of gold had reached other places, and soon ships from the Atlantic coast, Mexico, and all over the world began sailing into San Francisco Bay. In '49 the first steamer, the *California*, arrived from New York, and soon five thousand people were in San Francisco, where most of the supplies for the gold-fields had to be bought. Many of the newcomers lived in canvas tents or brush-covered shanties scattered about in the high sand-hills or in the thick chaparral. Some houses were built of adobe bricks, and the two-story frame Parker House was thought to be so fine that it rented for fifteen thousand dollars a month. Some wooden houses were brought out from the East in numbered pieces, like children's blocks, to be put together here, and others thought to be fireproof were of iron plates made in the East.

The first public school was opened in '48 and in the same building church services were held Sundays. The first post-office was in a store at the corner of Washington and Montgomery streets in '49. By 1850 the city had five square miles of land that had been cut down from sand-hills or filled in on the mud-flats. The houses along the city-front were built on piles, and the tide ebbed and flowed under them. Long wharves for the unloading of ships ran out into deep water. At Jackson and Battery streets a ship was used for a storehouse, and after the earth was filled in this stranded vessel was left standing among the houses. On Clay and Sansome streets the old hulk *Niantic* had a hotel upon her decks, and the first city prison was in the hold of the brig *Euphemia*.

While most of the miners were steady, hard-working men, honest, and very kind and generous to each other, some drank and gambled their hard-earned gold-dust away with a get of men who were ready to do any wrong thing for money. The gamblers and bad characters grew so troublesome by '51 that the police could do little or nothing with them. Every day some one was robbed, or murdered, and thieves often set fire to houses that they might plunder. As the judges and police could not control these criminals, nearly two hundred good citizens formed a "vigilance committee." It was agreed that bad characters should be told to leave town, and that robbers and murderers should be punished by the committee. Not long after, the vigilance committee hanged four men, and roughs and law-breakers left town for the mines. Men soon learned to keep the laws and do right.

Since almost all the houses in San Francisco were light frames of wood covered with cloth or paper, and since there was no fire department, there were six great fires, each of which nearly burnt up the town. The only way to stop the flames was to pull down houses or to blow them up with gunpowder. But almost before the ashes of one fire had cooled, wooden, cloth and paper buildings would cover whole blocks, to be burned again before long. The fifth great fire, in '51, destroyed a thousand houses and ten million dollars' worth of property in a night. One warehouse containing many barrels of vinegar was saved by covering the roof with blankets dipped in the vinegar, as no water could be had. The iron houses that had been thought fire-proof were of no use. Men who stayed in them found too late that the iron doors swelled with the heat and could not be opened, so that those within were smothered to death.

Then people began to guard against such fires by building new houses of stone or of brick. The sixth great fire destroyed most of the wooden buildings in the business part of the city. After that, with two or three fire companies and engines and better houses, people no longer dreaded the fire-bell. Water was piped into the city from Mountain Lake, and there was plenty for all purposes.

ENTRANCE TO JAPANESE
TEA GARDEN,
SAN FRANCISCO.
Click photo to see full-sized.

So the city grew larger, until in '53 there were fifty thousand people of all races and countries who called San Francisco home. Chinese and Japanese, the Mexican, African, Pacific Islander, Greek, or Turk, or Malay elbowed crowds of Americans, English, French, and Germans. It was said that any foreigner could find in the city those who spoke his language, and that gold was a word all knew.

The largest yield of gold from the mines was in '53, and the next year was a poor year for the miners. They bought fewer goods in San Francisco, and the storekeepers found business falling off. Too many houses had been built, so rents went down and times were hard for a year or two. In '55 there were many bank failures, and business troubles of all kinds made the people restless, and roughs and murderers carried a strong hand. Then the "law and order party," as the vigilance committee was at that time called, began once more the task of punishing those who robbed or killed. A list of criminal offenders was made out, and such were sent away from the state. One excellent result of the vigilance committee's labors was that a "people's party," as it was called, chose the best men to govern the city, and for years after peace and order were in San Francisco.

In '54 the city was lighted with gas for the first time, at a cost of fifteen dollars a thousand feet. In that year also the mint began to coin money from gold-dust, making five, ten and twenty-dollar pieces. Lone Mountain Cemetery was laid out about this time, and the old Yerba Buena graveyard, where the City Hall now stands, was closed.

San Francisco had, for some years, trouble about titles to property, owing to false or defective land-grants given by the Mexicans. Men tried to take possession of lots they had no real claim to by building a shanty on the ground and squatting there, and the "squatter troubles" between such land thieves and the rightful owners caused lawsuits and shooting affairs. A land commission finally settled these disputes, throwing out all the false claims and giving titles to the proper persons.

THE NEW CLIFF HOUSE,
SAN FRANCISCO.
Click photo to see full-sized.

The little village of Yerba Buena has now grown to be the largest city on the Pacific coast and one that is known the world over. It is widely and justly celebrated as the centre of great manufacturing and shipping interests, for its fine buildings, its climate, and its beautiful surroundings. San Francisco Bay, the harbor the Franciscans named for their patron saint, is noted for its picturesque scenery. Golden Gate Park, with its thousand acres of trees and lawn and flowers stretching out to the Pacific Ocean, the famous Cliff House, and the Golden Gate, through which so many Argonauts sailed into California, are the most attractive and best known places.

MEN CALIFORNIA REMEMBERS

Many pages of this book might be filled with California's roll of honor,—with that long list of men whose names are remembered whenever the state's history is recalled.

Explorers, Mission-builders, Argonauts, and pioneers were the men who helped to make California the fair state you know and live in. From the first day of the Spanish discoveries on this shore of the Pacific Ocean, we find brave and great men who gave their best efforts, and sometimes their lives, for California.

Let us head our brief list with Cortes, the name-giver, who dreamed long years of the golden land he was never to see. Then Cabrillo, the sea-king whom San Diego people honor every year because he found their bay and first set foot on California's ground. Next comes the bold Englishman, Sir Admiral Francis Drake, who intended that his queen, Elizabeth, should have this Indian kingdom, as he believed it to be. The stone Prayer-book Cross, in Golden Gate Park, was put up to commemorate the service of prayer and psalms, offered at Drake's Bay by Fletcher, the minister on the Admiral's ship.

Good Father Serra, the founder of the Missions, his friend and brother-priest Father Palou of San Francisco, and their fellow-laborers Crespi and Lasuen, helped in the work of building churches and teaching the Indians. Governor Portola, the first Spanish ruler of Alta California, assisted the Padres, and also found San Francisco Bay. Lieutenant Ayala, however, sailed the first ship, the *San Carlos*, through the Golden Gate. Another governor, de Neve, founded San José and Los Angeles, and wrote a set of laws for the two Californias of his time. That wise ruler, Governor Borica, ordered schools opened and tried to get the Indians to farm their lands and to raise hemp and flax.

Many of the old Spanish settlers and explorers have left us their names, though they are themselves forgotten, as Martinez, Amador, Castro, Bodega, and countless others plainly show. The Englishmen Livermore, Gilroy and Mark West, those early settlers, Temple and Rice at Los Angeles, Yount and Pope of Napa Valley, Don Timoteo Murphy of San Rafael, and Lassen the Dane, for whom Lassen's Peak was named, were among those who came here before 1830.

Governor Figueroa, called the "benefactor of Alta California" ordered the Missions to be given up to the Indians. By directing that the town of Yerba Buena should be laid out, he also is remembered as the founder of San

Francisco. Richardson, who carried out the governor's orders, was the first settler and Leese built the first frame-house of San Francisco.

In Governor Alvarado's time many Americans came to the new country, although Alvarado and General Vallejo tried hard to keep them out. Vallejo was then the military commander, and had headquarters at Sonoma, where he had an adobe fort and a few soldiers to protect the Mission of Solano. Here General Vallejo was living with his Indian and Californian settlers when the place was taken by Ide, the leader of the "bear-flag party." Vallejo, set free when the short-lived "bear-flag republic" went to pieces, lived many years at Sonoma. He was afterwards a member of the first legislature. He tried hard in 1851 to have the state capital at Vallejo; but he failed, for he did not keep his agreement to put up buildings for government use.

A man well known in the early days was John Sutter, a Swiss, who built a fort and settled where Sacramento now stands. He called his colony New Helvetia, and soon had about three hundred Indians at work for him. Some of the men were carpenters, blacksmiths, and farmers, while the women wove blankets or a coarse cloth. His fort enclosed about an acre of ground, with an adobe wall twenty feet high. A large gate was shut every night to keep safe those inside this walled fort. You have read that Marshall, who found gold, was building a sawmill for Sutter when he picked up the precious yellow nuggets. Sutter and Marshall quarrelled at last about the ownership of the mill at Coloma, where the pieces of gold were picked up. Marshall died a poor man, unhappy and neglected by the state, which has since put a costly bronze statue over his grave.

Sutter was very active in the Micheltorena war, when Governor Micheltorena was defeated and put out of office by Alvarado and Castro.

The last of the Mexican governors, Pio Pico, tried his best to prevent the rush of Americans into his country, but though Castro, the military commander, helped him, the Americans came and stayed. And both Pico and Castro with their soldiers were driven out of California at last by Fremont and Stockton.

General Fremont, the "path-finder," who could easily find the best way through a wilderness and could make maps or roads for others to follow him, is a striking figure in California history. He made three exploring trips to this coast, Kit Carson, the famous hunter and trapper, being his guide and scout. From the Oregon line to San Diego, Fremont knew the country. He was a brave Indian fighter and helped to capture California from Mexico. Fremont was appointed governor of the new territory by Stockton, and was the first senator from California representing the state in Congress. In 1848 Fremont sent a map of the country to Congress, and on it named the strait at the entrance to San Francisco Bay the Golden Gate. He was, therefore, the first to use this beautiful name now known the world over. His wife, Jessie Benton Fremont, is still living in Los Angeles.

Commodore Sloat, who raised the American flag at Monterey, and Commodore Stockton were United States naval officers who helped to conquer the Mexican and Indian forces with the aid of Fremont and General Kearny. These four men won the land of gold for the Union.

General John Bidwell, another "path-finder," who in 1841 led the first party of white men over the Sierras, lived to be over eighty years of age. He saw the state, once a wilderness where naked Digger Indians chased elk and antelope, grow to a pleasant land of orchards and vineyards, of great cities full of people. General Bidwell was for a time in Sutter's employ, and surveyed nearly all the large ranches and the roads in early days. All his life he planted trees and built roads, and at his great Rancho Chico is one of the largest orchards in the state. Part of his life-work was to help a tribe of savage Indians to be good American citizens, and as one of the fathers of California he should always be remembered.

Many notable names appear in the days when the finding of gold brought this shore of the Pacific Ocean before the eyes of the world. Among these are Gwin, who was chosen senator with Fremont; Larkin, widely known as the first and last American Consul to California and for his accounts of the gold discovery; and Halleck, first secretary of the state and afterward General Halleck.

The streets of San Francisco honor some of the citizens of 1848 and 1849: Geary, the first postmaster; Leavenworth and Hyde, the first alcaldes or mayors; Van Ness, Broderick, Turk, and McAllister, recalling prominent men of those days. Spanish families like Sanchez, Castro, Noe, Bernal, and Guerrero had also a place on the city map. Indeed, every town has some native Californian names in and around it.

Don Victor Castro, said to be the first white child born in San Francisco, died lately at San Pablo in the house he had built sixty years ago. He was called the last of the Spanish grandees, those dons who, before the Gringos came, had estates that stretched miles away on every hand, and thousands of cattle with many Indian servants. Don Victor built and ran the first ferry across San Francisco Bay.

Sacramento was laid out as a town for Sutter by three lieutenants of the U.S. army: Warner, who was afterwards killed by Indians; Ord, who was a general in the Civil War, while the third, in after years "marched through Georgia" as General Sherman. Marysville was also laid out by Sutter, and Stockton by Weber, who owned all the land around it.

In 1849 Doctor Gregg and his party found Humboldt Bay. In 1851 Yosemite Valley was discovered by Major Savage and a company of soldiers, who were out hunting hostile Indians. This band of Indians was called the Yosemites, and their old chief's name was Tenaya, for whom the beautiful lake is named.

Those who came to California before 1850 were called pioneers, and many of them built up great fortunes. Among them were Coleman, the president of the vigilance committee, Sharon, Flood, Fair, O'Brien, Tevis, Phelan, and James Lick. Lick was a remarkable man, who gave away an immense fortune; building the Lick Observatory, a school of mechanical arts, free public baths, an old ladies' home, and giving a million to the Academy of Science and the Society of California Pioneers.

In later days the names crowd thickly upon each other. Among editors and literary men the fearless and ill-fated James King of the *Evening Bulletin*, J. Ross Browne, the reporter of the first convention and a most interesting writer, Derby the humorist, "Caxton" or W.H. Rhodes, Mark Twain, Bret Harte, the historians Hittell and Bancroft, and the poet Joaquin Miller may be noted.

The governors of the state have been men remarkable as brilliant speakers or lawyers and as wise rulers. In 1875, during the time of Pacheco, the first native-born governor, the order of "Native Sons of the Golden West" was formed, which now numbers over ten thousand young California men. The "Native Daughters," a sister society, follows also the idea of keeping the love of California warm in the hearts of her children.

OUR GLORIOUS CLIMATE

Not only a glorious but in many ways a wonderful climate is enjoyed by the people of California's sea-coast and mountains, her valleys and foot-hills. In no other state can one find so many kinds of weather in such short distances. For instance, in Southern California you may pick flowers and oranges in almost tropical gardens, and in an hour find winter and throw snowballs on the high mountains overlooking the roses and orange groves you so lately left.

Only in the mountains, along that granite backbone of the state known as the Sierra Nevadas, are there four seasons, the spring, summer, autumn, and winter common to most of the United States. So the Sierras have a distinct climate of their own. The Sacramento and San Joaquin river valleys have another climate peculiar to themselves, while south of latitude 35 degrees the coast has less rain and is warmer than the coast counties north of that line.

In the greater part of the state the year is divided into a dry summer and a wet winter. The rains begin in October, and the first showers fall on dry, brown hills and dusty fields baked hard by steady sunshine since May. After these showers the grass springs up, and the fields are green almost as quickly as if some fairy godmother had waved her wand. An army of wild flowers, whose seeds were hidden in the brown earth, wakes when the rain-drops patter, and the plants get ready to bloom in a month or so. For this season, from November to February, with little frost and no ice nor snow, is winter in name only. Roses and violets bloom in the gardens and yellow poppies on the hills.

People expect and hope for much rain in this so-called winter, since a wet year assures good crops to the state. But the amount of rain that falls is very uncertain. It does not rain every day, nor all day, as a rule, and each storm seems different. Sometimes a "southeaster" blows up from the Japan Current, or Black Stream, as the Japanese call the warm, dark-blue waters that pour out of the China Sea. This current of the Pacific Ocean flows along our coast in a mighty river a thousand miles wide, and gives California its peculiar climate of cool summers and moist, warm winters. The southeasterly wind ruffles the bay with white-capped waves and dashes sheets of rain against window and roof. Then the wind changes, and all the clouds go flying to north or east, while from the clear blue sky brilliant sunshine pours down to make the grass and flowers grow. During the winter months the sun is strong and warm enough to make out-door life delightful.

The farmer depends greatly upon the rainfall. In a wet winter the moisture sinks far into the ground, but not so deep that the thirsty little roots cannot find it in the summer. Early rains are needed to soften the ground for November ploughing, and young grain and crops of all kinds need rain through April. In the northern part of the state the wet season begins earlier and lasts longer than in the south, while the southeastern corner is an almost rainless desert.

In San Francisco the thermometer seldom falls below 45° in the winter, the average for the season being 51°. Perhaps in January or February the sidewalks may be white with frost in the mornings, or hail may fall during some cold rain-storm. Once in five years or so, enough snow falls to make children go wild with delight over a few snowballs which are very soon melted. People can be comfortable the year round without fires, and the clear, bright winter days with soft air and warm sunshine are always pleasant enough to spend outdoors. This ocean climate, due to the warm sea air, is enjoyed by the counties facing the coast and San Francisco Bay. In the valleys of the interior white frosts are frequent, and thin ice forms on the wayside puddles. Once in a while killing frosts destroy fruit blossoms and cut down the garden flowers and vegetables, but seldom do more damage.

In mountain regions, above five or six thousand feet, the very cold winter lasts six or seven months. Snow falls almost constantly and drifts to a great depth. Small lakes are frozen and buried in snow, and the trees are bent and weighed down with ice and sleet. Many of the wild animals come down to the foot-hills below the snow-line to spend the winter; but the bear curls himself up in his warm cave and sleeps through the cold months. In this snowy zone of the Sierras, about thirty miles wide, winter lasts from the first snowfall, about the end of October, to the late spring of June. Then July and August are months of glorious weather, with clear, dry air and a cloudless sky. During the day the temperature of about 80 degrees melts much snow, and the rivers carry it away in rushing torrents and falls of icy water. In September the frost turns the leaves of all but the evergreen trees beautiful colors of red and yellow. Indian summer comes during September and October, when the days are sunny and warm, and then the long winter sets in again. Peaks above eight thousand feet are snow-clad on their crests and along their sides by deep drifts the year round.

Along the Pacific coast in summer cool sea-winds, called trade-winds, blow in from the ocean, and 60 degrees is the average temperature. The farther you go inland from the coast, the hotter it gets, and the heat is very great in the interior of the state. In the San Joaquin and Sacramento valleys it is often over 100 degrees in the shade, though this dry heat is not hard to bear, and the nights are always cool enough for one to sleep in comfort.

Summer fogs are usual in the coast counties. The mornings are pleasant and sunny till about eleven o'clock. At this time the sun's rays grow stronger in the interior valleys, and the hot air rises while trade-winds rush in from the cold ocean and fog settles down like a thick, gray cloud over the bay and hills. July and August are cold and foggy along the coastline, with strong west winds almost every day. In September the winds die away, and sometimes a shower or two falls.

The rainless desert, or southeastern corner of our state, is the hottest region of all. Here the sun glares down till sand and rocks seem heated by a fiery furnace. Every living creature gasps and pants for breath in the scorching heat. There are no trees, but only cactus, that queer, prickly, thorny plant, often fifteen or twenty feet high in these wastes of sand, and low greasewood bushes. Under this vegetation snakes, lizards, and horned toads bask all day and search for food at night. If travellers wander from the road in crossing the desert, they are easily lost, and sometimes they die or go mad in the terrible heat. There are no springs, and water stations are a long way apart, so that lost people usually die of thirst. As the heat of the sun's rays quivers over the burning sands, a curious sight called a mirage is often produced. A cool, glassy lake or flowing river bordered with green trees seems pictured in the air, and the hot and weary traveller can scarcely believe that only sand and rocks are before him.

Can you tell which season you like the best? You will find the one you choose in some part of this favored state. It is always summer in the south, and you may slide on the ice or throw snowballs all year in the high Sierras.

SOME WONDERFUL SIGHTS

California is a wonderland where snowy mountains, mighty and ancient forests, glaciers and geysers, lakes and waterfalls, foaming rivers and the cliffs and rolling surf down her long sea-coast give new and beautiful pictures at every place.

Through the whole state stretches the granite backbone of the Sierra Nevadas with its highest crest or ridge at the head-waters of the Kings and Kern rivers near Fresno. Here Mount Whitney and a dozen other great peaks of the High Sierras or California Alps lift their heads over thirteen thousand feet in the air. Here are to be seen most magnificent panoramas of lofty peaks, deep cañons, towering domes, and snow-clad summits. The finest forests, too, in the world grow on the slopes of the Sierras, the immense pines and giant *sequoias* of the General Grant and other National Parks in this section being the largest and oldest of all. Kings River cañon is a rugged gorge half a mile deep with the river rushing through it in thundering rapids and cascades.

"EL CAPITAN"
(3300 feet in height)
Click photo to see full-sized.

YOSEMITE FALLS.
Click photo to see full-sized.

The well-known Yosemite Valley is the gorge of the Merced River and, though only eight miles long and half a mile wide, holds the grandest of all our mountain scenery. The mighty rock El Capitan, over three thousand feet in height, stands at the entrance to the valley, and across from it is Bridal Veil Fall, a snowy cascade so thin you can see the face of the mountain through the falling waters. There are many waterfalls, but the Yosemite is chief of them all. Here the river takes a plunge of sixteen hundred feet, the water falling like snowy rockets bursting into spray from that great height.

Then, for six hundred feet more, the torrent leaps and foams through a trench it has cut out of the solid rock to the cliff, from which it takes a second plunge. This Lower Yosemite fall is four hundred feet high, the rushing waters turning into clouds of spray, which the wind tosses from side to side. At Nevada Fall the Merced River leaps six hundred feet at a bound, strikes a mass of rocks halfway down, and breaks into white foam upon which rainbows play when the sun shines through the misty veil.

Besides the grand Sentinel Rock, Eagle Peak, Clouds' Rest, and other high mountains in the Yosemite Valley, many domes or round-topped peaks like the heads of buried giants loom up, the most famous being South Dome, Washington Column, Liberty Cap, and Mount Broderick.

But no one can picture this wonderful valley with pen or brush or camera and give its real charm. You must see it yourself to know and understand the beauty of great mountains and falling waters, of Mirror Lake with its fine reflections of the surrounding scenery, and of the rushing torrent of the Merced River in its swift coursing through this mighty cañon of the Yosemite. Thousands of tourists and sightseers visit the valley from May to October. Then snow begins to fall and winter sets in, as it does everywhere in the high Sierras. Very deep snow-drifts cover the ground, lakes and rivers freeze, and the great falls are fringed with icicles, while a large ice cone forms at the foot of the falling water. Many beautiful pictures may be found in the valley in winter when Jack Frost is ruler of all the snow-clad, ice-bound cañon.

Scattered throughout the Sierras are other valleys almost as fine as the Yosemite. These are not often reached by the army of summer sight-seers, but true mountaineers find them. One valley which has fine scenery is the Grand cañon of the Tuolumne, the gorge being twenty-five miles long, with walls so high and steep that once entered one must go through to the end. The Tuolumne River rushes, with terrible force and speed, in cascades and rapids down the granite stairway which is the floor of this cañon. The walls of the gorge rise so high that the traveller only sees a tiny strip of blue sky far above him, and the great pine trees on top of these cliff walls seem only the length of one's finger.

It is supposed that all these valleys have been formed by glaciers, which during the ice age, thousands of years ago, filled the cañons and swept over the mountains. These masses of ice, moving very slowly, ground and tore up the rocks under and around them till deep gorges and steep, high cliffs were left in their tracks. Most of the glaciers melted long ago, but on Mount Lyell, on Shasta, and a few of the Sierra summits may still be found those ever-living ice-rivers, the one on Mount Lyell being the source of the Tuolumne River.

California is rich in lakes, especially in the mountains where the melting snows gather in every hollow and form lakelets in chains or groups, or in one large body of water like Tahoe, Donner, or Tenaya lakes.

One of the most beautiful lakes in the world is Lake Tahoe. It is six thousand feet above sea-level, and the mountains around it rise four thousand feet higher. On these peaks snow-drifts lie the year round above the "snow-line," as a height over eight or nine thousand feet is called. Nevada, treeless and barren, is on the eastern side of Lake Tahoe, while the western or California side is green and thickly wooded with beautiful pines. But the first thing one would notice, perhaps, is the wonderful clearness of the lake water. As one stands on the wharf the steamer *Tahoe* seems to be hanging in the clear green depths with her keel and twin propellers in plain sight. The fish dart under her and all about as in some large aquarium. There a big lake-trout shoots by like a silver streak of light, or here is a school of hundreds of little fingerlings. Every stick or stone shows on the bottom as one starts out on the steamer, and as one sails along where the water is sixty or seventy feet deep. In the middle the lake's depth is fifteen hundred feet and the water is a dark indigo-blue. At the edge and along shallow places the color is bright green, as at Emerald Bay, a beautiful inlet three miles long. Lake Tahoe is twenty miles in length and about five wide, and its icy cold waters are of crystal clearness and very pure.

FALLEN LEAF LAKE.
Click photo to see full-sized.

Fallen Leaf Lake is a smaller Tahoe, and Donner Lake, not far from Truckee, and now the camping-place of many a summer visitor, is the place where years ago the Donner overland party spent a terrible winter in the Sierra snows.

Clear Lake and the Blue Lakes in Lake County are delightful places to visit, and in this county, too, are the geysers. Some wonderful curiosities are seen here. You will find springs that spout up a stream of hot water every few minutes, mineral springs from which you can have a drink of soda water, and an acid spring that flows lemonade. Alum, iron, or sulphur waters, either hot or cold, bubble up out of the ground at every turn. At one spring you may boil an egg. Other springs are used for steam baths and also hot mud-baths. In Geyser cañon is the strange place every sight-seer hurries to at once. Such rumblings and thunderings, such hot vapors and gases come from the cracks in the ground, that the Indians thought this was the workshop where the bad spirit which white people call the devil used to live and work. The deeper one goes into this cañon, the hotter and noisier it gets. All round are signs telling where it is dangerous to step, while the ground is hot, and boiling water runs by in little streams. Steam rises from many pools, and the sulphur smell almost chokes one. Another curious spring, called the devil's inkstand, seems full of ink. Mount St. Helena, near here, is a dead or extinct volcano, and probably there are fires in the earth under this region which keep up these steam and sulphur springs.

MOUNT SHASTA FROM
STRAWBERRY VALLEY.
Click photo to see full-sized.

Many of the Sierra summits are capped with volcanic rock, and Lassen's Peak and Mount Shasta are extinct volcanoes. There are hot springs and cracks from which steam and sulphur rise on both of these mountains, and as earthquakes often shake the earth in different parts of the state we know that underground fires are still at work. A great piece of land on Mount San Jacinto in Southern California lately sank down about a hundred feet, and cracks both deep and wide show that some force from below gave a thorough shaking-up to that part of the state.

Mono, Owen's, and several other large lakes are the "sinks" into which rivers flow and lose themselves in the sandy or marshy shores. These lakes have soda or salt in their waters, and great stretches of dry alkali lands around them. The famous Death Valley is a dry lake of this kind where the sun beats down on the white alkali plain till it is almost certain death to try to cross it without a guide. The Salton Sea is a dry lake where almost pure salt is dug out, and great quantities of borax and of soda are found in other beds, of dried-up streams and lakes.

But to tell of all the curious things nature has to show us in California,—of the forests of petrified trees, of the caverns cut out of the ocean cliffs by restless waves, or of those in the mountains or the Modoc lava-beds,—well, you will see most of them, let us hope, in your vacations. A large book might be given to the wonderful sights of this great state, and it may be your fortune to visit and so always remember a few we have named.

Milton Keynes UK
Ingram Content Group UK Ltd.
UKHW030719041024
449263UK00004B/366